THE CHANGING WORLD

OCEANS & RIVERS

DR FRANCES DIPPER

THUNDER BAY
P·R·E·S·S

Code of Safety

All activities should be conducted under adult supervision. Most of the habitats described in this series are dangerous because they are at the extremes of how our world works. They are not places you should visit without preparation or without a qualified guide. You should take suitable equipment and wear the right clothing for the environment. Take a map and a compass on all trips and learn how to use them properly. If you should find yourself in such a place through an accident, you will find some tips on how to survive there on page 67.

- **Before you go on a trip**, plan your route. **Always** tell an adult where you are going and when you expect to return.
- **Always go with a friend**, and preferably go as a party of four, which is a safe minimum number.

   If possible, go with at least one adult whom you trust—ideally someone who knows the area and the subject you are studying.
- **Ask permission** before going on to private property.
- **Leave gates closed or open** depending on how you find them. Keep off crops and avoid damaging soils, plants, animals, fences, walls, and gates.
- **Take your litter home** or dispose of it properly.
- **Remember** that many plants and animals, and their homes and habitats, are protected by law.
- **Ask your parents** not to light fires except in an emergency.
- **Beware of natural hazards** such as slippery slopes, crumbling cliffs, loose rocks, rotten tree trunks and branches, soft mud, deep water, swift currents, and tides.
- **Beware of poisonous berries**, plants, and animals: if you are not sure, don't touch them.
- Remember: **if in doubt, always play safe.**

Picture Credits

The Enviromental Picture Library: 63. Kevin Madison: 6/7; 8/9; 18/19; 22; 27; 30/31; 64/65. Mary Evans Picture Library: 63. Rex Features; 24. Mike Saunders: 8/9; 10/11; 12/13; 14/15; 17; 20/21; 24/25; 28/29; 36/37; 44/45. Science Photo Library: back cover, endpapers, 1 (© Tom Van Sant, Geosphere Project, Santa Monica). Michael Shoebridge: 23; 26. Wildlife Art Agency: (Brin Edwards) 39, 40/41, 42/43, 46/47, 50/51, 58/59; (Darren Harvey) 54/55, 56/57, 62/63; (Steve Roberts) 32, 33, 52/53, 65; (Chris Turnbull) 34/35. Activity pictures by Mr Gay Galsworthy.

Thunder Bay Press
5880 Oberlin Drive, Suite 400
San Diego, CA 92121

First published in the United States and Canada by Thunder Bay Press, 1996

© Dragon's World Ltd, 1996
© Text Frances Dipper, 1996
© Illustrations by specific artists, 1996

Editor	Diana Briscoe
Series Editor	Steve Parker
Designer	Martyn Foote
Art Director	John Strange
Design Assistants	Karen Ferguson
	Victoria Furbisher
DTP Manager	Michael Burgess
Editorial Director	Pippa Rubinstein

Library of Congress Cataloging-in-Publication Data
Dipper, Frances. 1951–
      Oceans & rivers.
      p.   cm. — (The changing world)
      Includes index.
      Summary: Looks at the element that covers nearly three-quarters of our planet, and describes the water cycle, ocean waves and river currents, and the threat that human carelessness and exploitation pose.
      ISBN 1–57145–027–0
      1. Ocean—Juvenile literature.
      2. Rivers—Juvenile literature.
      [1. Ocean.   2. Rivers.]
I. Title   II. Series: Changing world (San Diego, Calif.)
GC21.5.D57   1996
551.46—dc20
                                                    96–5009
                                                    CIP
                                                    AC

Typeset by Dragon's World Ltd in Garamond, Caslon 540 and Frutiger.
Printed in Italy

Contents

The Changing World of
Oceans and Rivers

Our world, planet Earth, has never been still since it first formed—4,600 million years ago. It goes around the Sun once each year, to bring the changing seasons. It spins like a top once each day, causing the cycle of day and night. Our close companion, the Moon, circles the Earth and produces the rise and fall of the ocean tides. The weather alters endlessly, too. Winds blow, water ripples into waves, clouds drift, rain falls, and storms brew. Land and sea are heated daily by the Sun, and cool or freeze at night.

Living on the Earth, we notice these changes on different time scales. First and fastest is our own experience of passing time, as seconds merge into minutes and hours. We move about, eat and drink, learn and play, rest and sleep. Animals do many of these activities, too.

Second is the longer, slower time scale of months and years. Many plants grow and change over these longer time periods. Return to a natural place after many years, and you see how some of the trees have grown, while others have died and disappeared.

Third is the very long, very slow time scale lasting hundreds, thousands and millions of years. The Earth itself changes over these immense periods. New mountains thrust up as others wear down. Rivers alter their course. One sea fills with sediments, but huge earth movements and continental drift create another sea elsewhere.

The *CHANGING WORLD* series describes and explains these events—from the immense time span of lands and oceans, to the shorter changes among trees and flowers, to the daily lives of ourselves and other animals. Each book in the series selects one feature or habitat of nature to reveal in detail. Here you can read how *OCEANS AND RIVERS* were formed, and how they continue to change today. You can find out about the many fascinating plants and animals which make their homes there, from microscopic seaweeds to giant blue whales.

MORE, AND MORE, AND ...

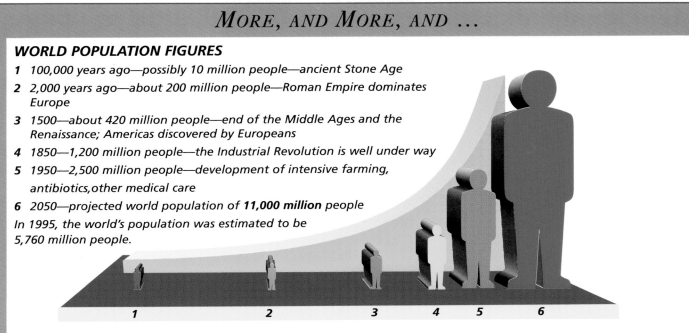

WORLD POPULATION FIGURES

1 100,000 years ago—possibly 10 million people—ancient Stone Age
2 2,000 years ago—about 200 million people—Roman Empire dominates Europe
3 1500—about 420 million people—end of the Middle Ages and the Renaissance; Americas discovered by Europeans
4 1850—1,200 million people—the Industrial Revolution is well under way
5 1950—2,500 million people—development of intensive farming, antibiotics,other medical care
6 2050—projected world population of **11,000 million** people

In 1995, the world's population was estimated to be 5,760 million people.

The most numerous large animal on Earth, by many millions, is the human. Our numbers have increased steadily from the start of civilization about 10,000 years ago, speeded by advances in public health and hygiene, the Industrial Revolution, gas and diesel engines, better farming, and better medical care.

However, this massive growth in humanity means that almost half the world's people suffer from hunger, poverty, and disease. The animals and plants who share our planet also suffer. As we expand our territory, their natural areas shrink ever faster. We probably destroy one species of plant or animal every week.

However, there is another type of change affecting our world. It is the huge and ever-increasing number of humans on the planet. The CHANGING WORLD series shows how we have completely altered vast areas—to grow foods, put up homes and other buildings, mine metals and minerals, manufacture goods and gadgets from pencils to washing machines, travel in cars, trains and planes, and generally live in our modern world.

This type of change is causing immense damage. We take over natural lands and wild places, forcing plants and animals into ever smaller areas. Some of them disappear for ever. We produce all kinds of garbage, waste, poisons, and water and air pollution.

However, there is hope. More people are becoming aware of the problems. They want to stop the damage, to save our planet, and to plan for a brighter future. The CHANGING WORLD series shows how we can all help. We owe it to our Earth, and to its millions of plants, animals, and other living things, to make a change for the better.

A Watery World

When you visit the seaside and look out over the waves, you get a tiny glimpse of our world's biggest habitat. More than two-thirds of the Earth is covered by water. More than 99.99 per cent of this water is salty—sea water. The fresh water in rivers and lakes makes up only a tiny proportion, 0.001 per cent, of the total water on our planet.

The oceans, and especially at their darkest depths, are the last great unexplored regions of our world. However, scientists are always developing new craft and machines, so that we can discover more about seas and oceans. How were they made?

Seas and oceans
Oceans are big, seas are smaller. Together, they contain 330 million cubic miles of water. The Earth's Southern Hemisphere (bottom half) is mostly ocean. The Northern Hemisphere has much more land.

Arctic Ocean
This is by far the smallest ocean, covering 5.5 million square miles. It is also much the shallowest, with an average depth of 4,375 feet. At its center is a great floating ice raft, the Arctic ice sheet.

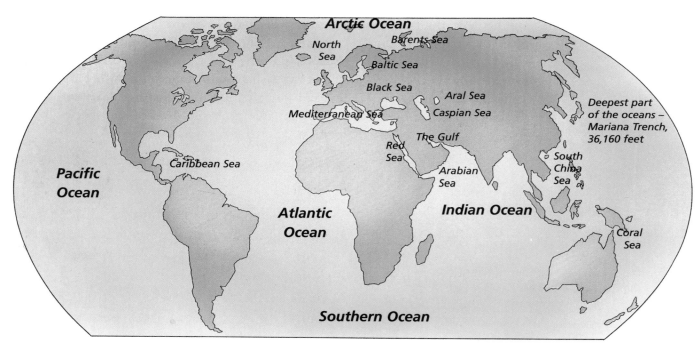

Pacific Ocean
The immense Pacific covers almost half of the globe, with an area of 64 million square miles. It is also the deepest ocean, with an average depth of 14,100 feet.

Atlantic Ocean
This is sometimes divided into two oceans, North Atlantic and South Atlantic. The total area is 32 million square miles. On average, the Atlantic is 12,140 feet deep.

Indian Ocean
The warmest of the oceans, the Indian Ocean has an area of 28 million square miles and an average depth of 12,800 feet. It contains about one quarter of all the world's sea water.

How have they changed through time? Which plants and animals live there? We are also discovering how rivers, lakes and oceans are changing in the modern world. They are being used as a global sewer, to dump home garbage and industrial refuse. They are polluted by chemicals and radioactive wastes, and damaged by many other human activities. We need to find out how to protect our rivers and oceans, and save our watery world for the future.

Salty and fresh

Almost any natural body of water has substances dissolved in it. The fresh water of streams, ponds, rivers, and lakes has small amounts of dissolved minerals. Sea water has lots more. Leave some sea water in a dish to dry, and you are left with fine, white, powdery crystals. This is salt—what chemists call sodium chloride—NaCl. It is also called

Planet "Ocean"
From space, the Earth looks mainly blue, because more than two-thirds of its surface is covered by water. When sunlight hits water, most of the colors in it are absorbed, and only blue is reflected. This view is centered on Japan and shows how the Pacific Ocean dominates that side of the Earth.

common salt, rock salt, and of course, sea salt. No one knows how this salt got into sea water. It may have been there from the very beginning, when seas and oceans first formed on our planet, more than 4,600 million years ago.

Some salt is worn away from rocks and soil and washed down rivers, into the sea. The saltiness or "salinity" of water is measured in parts per thousand (ppt), that is how many units of sodium chloride there are in a thousand units of water. The usual salinity of the sea is about 35 ppt. The saltiest sea is the Dead Sea, between Israel and Jordan. It is not joined to any other seas and oceans. Salts and minerals wash into the Dead Sea, and pure water evaporates from it in the hot climate, so this sea has got steadily saltier. It is now so salty, at 260 ppt, that nothing can live there. The salt makes the water so dense that you can float without trying!

SHRINKING SEAS

Millions of years ago, the Tethys Sea covered a vast area. As the land around it rose, it gradually shrank and split into three main seas – the Black, Caspian and Aral Seas. Even in the past 40 years, the Aral Sea has shrunk by one-fifth, its water taken for surrounding farmland. Towns once on its shore are now 31 miles inland.

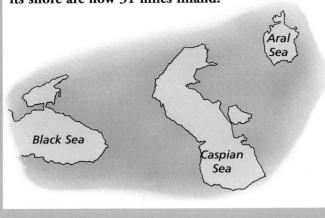

Rivers of the World

A river is a ribbon of water flowing downhill. It begins or rises at its source, which may be a small spring spurting from the ground, or a massive lake in the hills, fed by heavy rains. Precipitation, the overall name for rain, hail, snow, and other forms of water coming from the air to the ground, keeps the river fed. However, not all rivers flow steadily all year. Some swell and flood in spring, as warmth melts ice and snow in the surrounding hills. Others dry up in summer, when there is no rain.

Smaller streams and rivers that flow into the main river are known as tributaries. Many rivers become wider at their end, forming a river mouth or estuary as they flow into a lake or sea. Some rivers run into the desert, trickling into the sand, like the Okavango in south-western Africa. Rivers have their own life, such as water weeds and fish. But all animals and plants need water, so rivers are often lined with trees and flowers, and they attract land animals which come to drink.

The top ten rivers

The Amazon is not the longest river in the world. But it is so wide and deep that it contains more water than the other six biggest rivers added together. Lake Baikal in Russia is the deepest lake in the world, at 5,708 feet, and holds one-fifth of the world's fresh water. The largest lake by area is Lake Superior in North America, at 32,150 square miles.

1 Nile
The world's longest river flows mainly through the deserts of Sudan and Egypt, in north-east Africa, into the Mediterranean Sea. Its total length is 4,157 miles.

2 Amazon
By far the biggest river in water volume, and 4,080 miles long, the Amazon flows through South American rainforests into the Atlantic.

3 Mississippi
With its huge tributary, the Missouri, the 3,740-mile Mississippi empties into the Gulf of Mexico.

4 Chang jiang (Yangtze)
At 3,715 miles, this is Asia's longest watercourse. It reaches the East China Sea at the port of Shanghai.

5 Yenisei
Flowing across the cold, marshy plains of Siberia, this 3,450-mile river is frozen for part of the year.

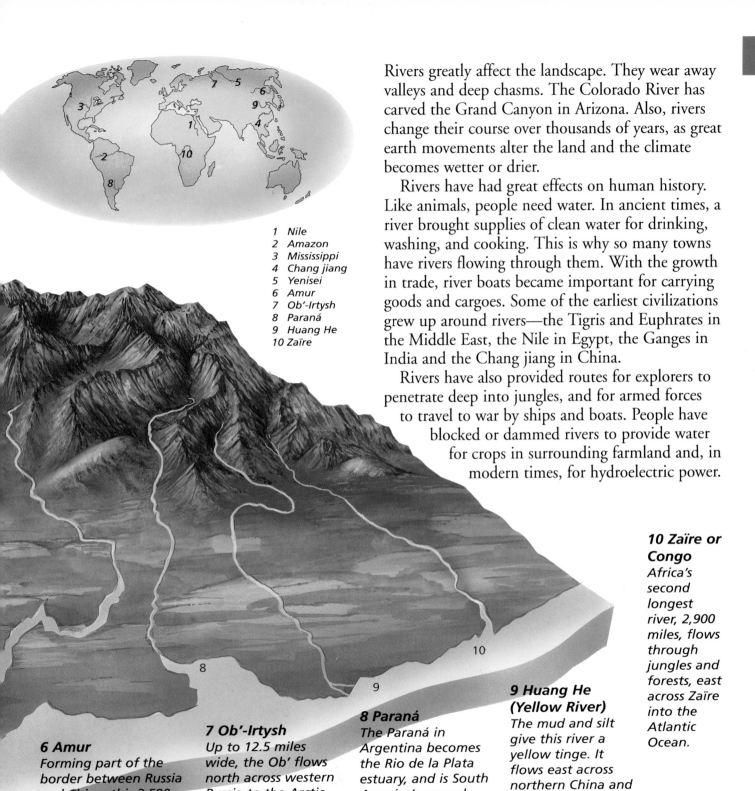

Rivers greatly affect the landscape. They wear away valleys and deep chasms. The Colorado River has carved the Grand Canyon in Arizona. Also, rivers change their course over thousands of years, as great earth movements alter the land and the climate becomes wetter or drier.

Rivers have had great effects on human history. Like animals, people need water. In ancient times, a river brought supplies of clean water for drinking, washing, and cooking. This is why so many towns have rivers flowing through them. With the growth in trade, river boats became important for carrying goods and cargoes. Some of the earliest civilizations grew up around rivers—the Tigris and Euphrates in the Middle East, the Nile in Egypt, the Ganges in India and the Chang jiang in China.

Rivers have also provided routes for explorers to penetrate deep into jungles, and for armed forces to travel to war by ships and boats. People have blocked or dammed rivers to provide water for crops in surrounding farmland and, in modern times, for hydroelectric power.

1 Nile
2 Amazon
3 Mississippi
4 Chang jiang
5 Yenisei
6 Amur
7 Ob'-Irtysh
8 Paraná
9 Huang He
10 Zaïre

10 Zaïre or Congo
Africa's second longest river, 2,900 miles, flows through jungles and forests, east across Zaïre into the Atlantic Ocean.

9 Huang He (Yellow River)
The mud and silt give this river a yellow tinge. It flows east across northern China and is 3,010 miles long.

8 Paraná
The Paraná in Argentina becomes the Rio de la Plata estuary, and is South America's second-longest waterway, at 3,032 miles.

7 Ob'-Irtysh
Up to 12.5 miles wide, the Ob' flows north across western Russia to the Arctic Ocean. It is 3,360 miles long and frozen half the year.

6 Amur
Forming part of the border between Russia and China, this 3,590-mile river flows into the Tartar Strait, Sea of Okhotsk.

9

The Water Cycle

Rain falling today may have fallen long before, on your grandparents, and even on dinosaurs millions of years ago! Nature has developed a very efficient recycling system for our water. The same water goes round and round in a process called the water cycle.

In warm weather, water from the oceans, rivers, and lakes slowly evaporates—changes into an invisible gas called water vapor. It leaves any salt and other minerals behind, so the vapor is fresh, not salty. As it rises into the sky, the water vapor cools and turns back into tiny water droplets, which form clouds. As the droplets get bigger they fall as rain, or as snow in colder places. This means that much of our rain comes from the sea.

Droplets fall as rain or freeze as snow and hail.

Plants and animals give off water vapor.

Water vapor rises, cools, and condenses, forming clouds of droplets.

Water evaporates from seas as invisible water vapor.

Water going round
Water evaporates from seas, lakes and rivers, and rises into the atmosphere. It is colder up there, so the water vapor cools and condenses back into water droplets or crystals, which fall as rain, hail, and snow. Much of this water runs into rivers and eventually back into the sea.

Water sinks through rocks such as chalk and collects deep below the surface as ground water.

Water evaporates from rivers and lakes as invisible water vapor.

Rain drains into rivers and lakes.

Rivers carry water back to the sea.

The seas also affect our weather, because of the way water absorbs warmth. When the sun shines, it warms up the land and the sea. But the sea takes much longer to warm up. The sea also loses its heat back into the air much more slowly, and spreads much of it around the world in ocean currents. This does not happen on the land. The result is that the difference in temperature between various oceans through the year is much less than the difference in temperatures on land through the seasons. There is only about 90°F difference between the coldest and the warmest parts of the ocean. On land, the difference is more than 200°F.

These differences in temperature between land and sea can affect wind direction and climate, make fogs, and cause rain. This means that a city by the sea has a much milder climate, with fewer extremes of temperature, than one far inland. Denver, Colerado, and Reno, Nevada, are about the same distance from the Equator (the same "latitude"). But Denver is far inland, away from any sea. So it has much colder winters, when snow and ice lie on the ground. This hardly ever happens in Reno.

Deeper, darker, colder and heavier
Surface temperatures of tropical oceans, warmed by the sun, may be more than 86°F. But deeper down, away from the sun, the temperature falls. Below about 3,280 feet, the temperature in all the oceans is usually 39–44.5°F. Pressure increases with depth too, as the weight of water above increases.

Surface zone
0–656 feet, warm and light, plenty of plants and living creatures

Bathyal zone
656–6,560 feet, twilight with cool water, few microscopic plants, some living creatures

Abyssal zone
Below 6,560 feet, pitch black, cold, fewer living creatures

11

Waves and Water Clarity

Waves are made by wind. It blows along the surface and piles up water as ripples, which gradually grow into larger waves. Some lakes are big enough to get quite rough in stormy weather. But only in the sea and the American Great Lakes can winds whip up really big waves.

The size of the waves depends on how far the wind has blown over open water. This is called the fetch. Hurricane-force winds can make waves 100 feet high—as tall as a 10-story building! Waves caused by storms in the Indian Ocean can reach Alaska, 12,430 miles away. Different oceans and seas have different wave features. The Mediterranean Sea is usually calm, with blue, placid water. The stormy North Sea, swept by many winds, has only a few really calm days each year.

Breakers
As a wave reaches shallow water it piles up into a sharp peak, then topples over. This is called breaking.

Ripples
On a calm, windless day there are hardly any waves, perhaps just a few small ripples.

Water movement
In waves, water particles move in circles. So a surface object bobs up and down; it only moves along if blown by wind.

Tsunami
A tsunami can surge several miles inland, causing immense damage and flooding land with salty sea water that ruins crops.

Swell
As the wind increases in speed and strength, it piles up water into regular humps, called a swell.

Water clarity
The clearness, or clarity, of water is affected by many factors, including temperature, winds, waves, and the nature of the seabed. If the bottom is mud or silt, waves, stir up these tiny particles and make the water turbid or cloudy. Scientists measure water clarity with a white plastic Secchi disc. You lower the disc into the water, and measure the depth at which you can no longer see it clearly.

Calm tropical seas are clear and blue.

Stormy European coastal waters are often brown.

Tiny plants and animals (plankton) grow well in coastal waters, making it cloudy and green or yellow.

Types of waves
The movement of wind over the sea's surface creates waves, which shape and change our coastlines. Waves break on the shore when they reach water that is shallower than their wavelength—the distance from one wave peak to the next.

As the hump-like waves called a swell move into shallower water, they begin to pile higher, then they topple over or "break" with a foaming crash. The slope of the beach, the size of the waves approaching it, and the wind and current conditions at the time all affect how large the breaking waves will be. Some beaches have regular large breakers and are popular with surfers.

The biggest waves are far too large and dangerous for surfing. They are sometimes called tidal waves, but they are not caused by tides, or even by winds. The proper name is "tsunami" and they are caused by earthquakes and volcanic eruptions on the sea bed. Most tsunamis occur in the Pacific, because this is the main area for seabed volcanoes and earthquakes. A tsunami can travel across the ocean as fast as a plane—405 miles per hour. In 1960, a single tsunami travelled 9,940 miles across the Pacific Ocean from Chile to Japan. In 1755, a tsunami swept many yards up the River Tagus in Portugal, causing many deaths.

Ocean Currents

Standing on the land, we can feel the air moving past us as wind. Winds at various heights blow in different speeds and directions. In the oceans, water moves in a similar way, but much more slowly. These are ocean currents—"underwater winds."

Currents circulate around all the main oceans. For example, a patch of water near the edge of the North Atlantic Ocean goes all the way round this ocean in ten years. Some currents flow at the

The Gulf Stream
The Gulf Stream was first described accurately by American scientist and statesman Benjamin Franklin, in the 1770s. It carries warm water from the Caribbean area to Northern Europe.

Main ocean currents
The main currents of the Atlantic Ocean have been mapped accurately by ships with special equipment, and also by satellites whose infrared cameras detect water at different temperatures. The bluer the arrows, the cooler the water.

surface while others move deeper down. It is estimated that all the water in the world's oceans, even near the deepest seabed, is moved around every 10,000 years. Scientists have worked out the speed and path of each surface current using drift bottles with notes in them. Today, they use modern electronic current meters which can be lowered on lines to various depths.

Ocean currents are caused by winds, by the warming effects of the sun on the water's surface, by changes in air pressure and by cold water rising up from the depths of the ocean as even colder water sinks down. In addition to the main oceanic currents, there are smaller currents near the coast, caused by the shape of the local shoreline and water

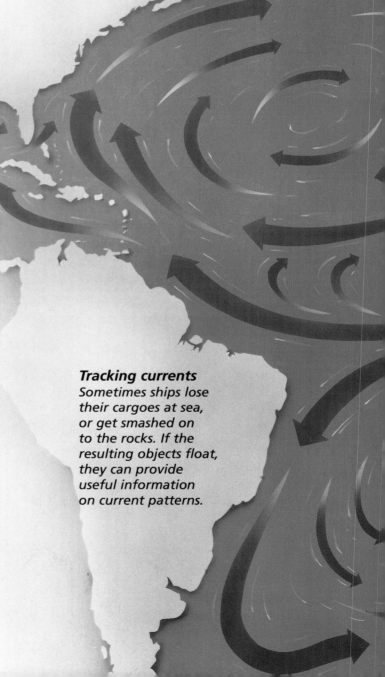

Tracking currents
Sometimes ships lose their cargoes at sea, or get smashed on to the rocks. If the resulting objects float, they can provide useful information on current patterns.

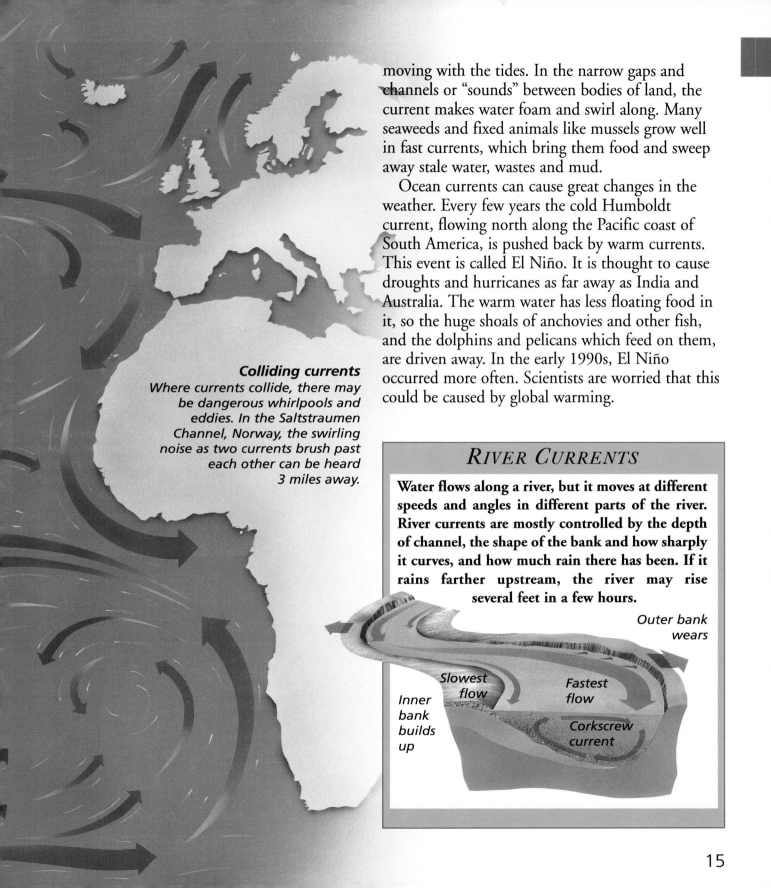

moving with the tides. In the narrow gaps and channels or "sounds" between bodies of land, the current makes water foam and swirl along. Many seaweeds and fixed animals like mussels grow well in fast currents, which bring them food and sweep away stale water, wastes and mud.

Ocean currents can cause great changes in the weather. Every few years the cold Humboldt current, flowing north along the Pacific coast of South America, is pushed back by warm currents. This event is called El Niño. It is thought to cause droughts and hurricanes as far away as India and Australia. The warm water has less floating food in it, so the huge shoals of anchovies and other fish, and the dolphins and pelicans which feed on them, are driven away. In the early 1990s, El Niño occurred more often. Scientists are worried that this could be caused by global warming.

Colliding currents
Where currents collide, there may be dangerous whirlpools and eddies. In the Saltstraumen Channel, Norway, the swirling noise as two currents brush past each other can be heard 3 miles away.

RIVER CURRENTS

Water flows along a river, but it moves at different speeds and angles in different parts of the river. River currents are mostly controlled by the depth of channel, the shape of the bank and how sharply it curves, and how much rain there has been. If it rains farther upstream, the river may rise several feet in a few hours.

Outer bank wears

Slowest flow

Fastest flow

Inner bank builds up

Corkscrew current

Is All Water the Same?

Water from a tap or mineral-water bottle is usually clear, colorless, and odorless. But what about water where animals and plants live, in nature? If you look at water from various sources, you soon see that it is not all the same! (Ask an adult to help you when taking water from ponds and barrels. Never put your wet fingers in your mouth.)

1 Collect samples of water from various places. You'll need a set of clear plastic containers, a small plastic jug, a thermometer, pen and notepad, plus an adult to help you.

2 Try the kitchen cold tap, the bath faucet, bottled water, and water from a rain barrel, a small stream, a pond, and a lake. As you take each sample, measure and note its temperature. Label each container.

3 Put the samples in similar containers, in a row. Let them settle. Look for any hint of color, and note this. Shake each sample; does it become cloudy? For how long?

4 Pour a little of each sample on to a white saucer. Label and leave them all together in a sunny place until they dry and disappear. Note what's left—grit, sand, dirt, dust, or stains.

5 Compare results. Depending on where it comes from, water may be warm, cool, clear, cloudy, or colored. It may have dissolved minerals that only show as it dries.

Are YOU a Water-waster?

When you wash or clean your teeth, do you ever think about how much water your family uses each day? If your water is metered, you have the answer straight away. If not, then use the chart to work out how much water is used in your house on a normal day. Divide this by the number of people living in the house for the number of pints per person.

Bathroom sink (full) • 9 pints
Tooth-cleaning (faucet running) • 3.5 pints
Cup of tea, lemonade, or similar • 0.5 pints
Garden hose • 17.5 pints per minute
Washing machine • 194 pints
Washing dishes by hand • 10.5 pints
Washing hands • 1 pint
Cooking • Measure the pan!
Full watering can • 9 pints
Full bucket • 14 pints
Dishwasher • 97 pints
Shower • 62 pints
Bath • 140 pints

How are YOU doing?

Water used per person each day

☺ 195 pints or less: Very good

☺ 195-230 pints: Quite good

☺ 230-300 pints: Average, room for improvement

☹ 300-335 pints: A bit wasteful, try harder

☹ 335 pints or more: A water-waster—try much harder!

The Changing Oceans

The Earth's oceans and land have not always been where they are now. They have been forming and changing for billions of years, and they are still changing today—very slowly. For example, the Atlantic Ocean gets wider each year, by about the width of a thumb. This is due to continental drift. The strong outer "skin" of the Earth, called the lithosphere, is like a cracked eggshell made up of about twelve large pieces. These are called tectonic plates. Some plates have oceans on them, others have landmasses, and some have both. The plates slide along over the deeper layers of the Earth, known as the mantle. The main continents and landmasses ride piggyback on their plates. And over millions of years, the oceans change shape.

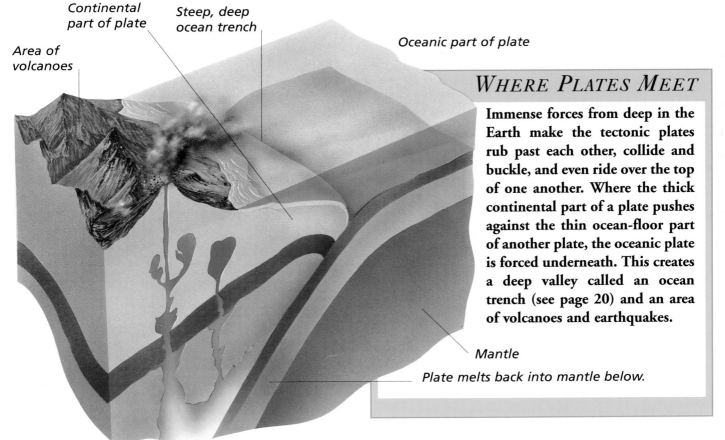

Continental part of plate

Steep, deep ocean trench

Oceanic part of plate

Area of volcanoes

Mantle

Plate melts back into mantle below.

WHERE PLATES MEET

Immense forces from deep in the Earth make the tectonic plates rub past each other, collide and buckle, and even ride over the top of one another. Where the thick continental part of a plate pushes against the thin ocean-floor part of another plate, the oceanic plate is forced underneath. This creates a deep valley called an ocean trench (see page 20) and an area of volcanoes and earthquakes.

Oceans of Time

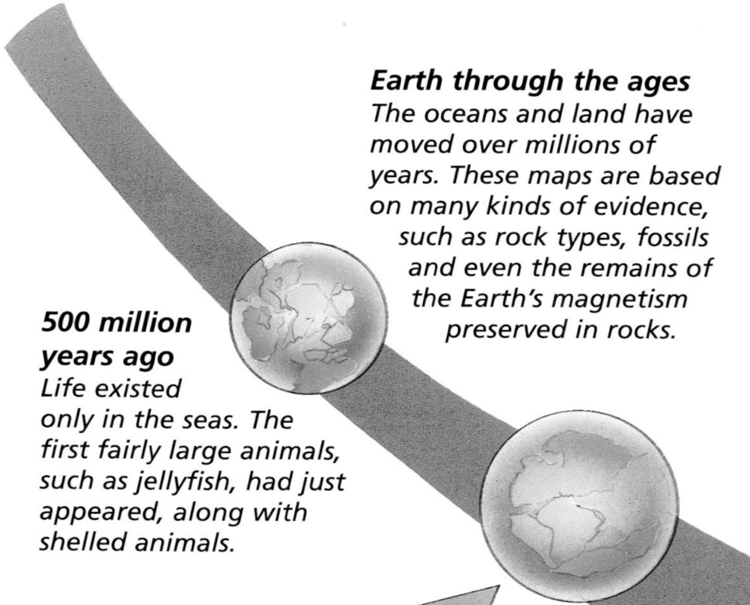

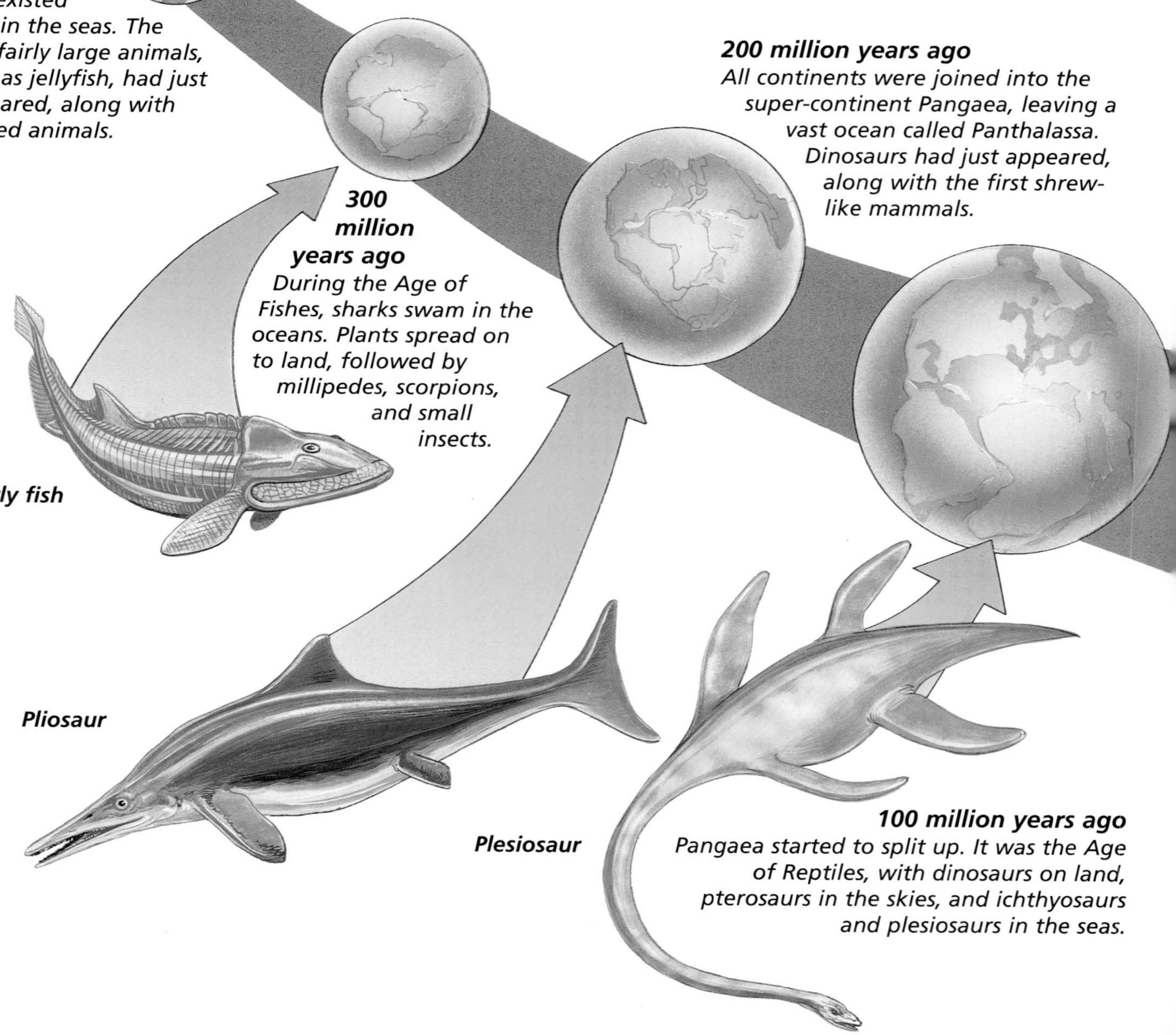

Earth through the ages
The oceans and land have moved over millions of years. These maps are based on many kinds of evidence, such as rock types, fossils and even the remains of the Earth's magnetism preserved in rocks.

We will probably never know exactly how oceans and continents were made. However, scientists have recently collected more evidence to support their theories, using drills which are several thousand feet long! Since 1968, they have been carrying out ocean-drilling projects. Using special research ships, they have drilled hundreds of feet into the sea floor, which is already thousands of feet below the ship on

500 million years ago
Life existed only in the seas. The first fairly large animals, such as jellyfish, had just appeared, along with shelled animals.

300 million years ago
During the Age of Fishes, sharks swam in the oceans. Plants spread on to land, followed by millipedes, scorpions, and small insects.

200 million years ago
All continents were joined into the super-continent Pangaea, leaving a vast ocean called Panthalassa. Dinosaurs had just appeared, along with the first shrew-like mammals.

Early fish

Pliosaur

Plesiosaur

100 million years ago
Pangaea started to split up. It was the Age of Reptiles, with dinosaurs on land, pterosaurs in the skies, and ichthyosaurs and plesiosaurs in the seas.

18

the surface. Samples of mud and rocks have been collected from many hundreds of sites. Some are more than 150 million years old. From them, and from the minerals and fossils they contain, scientists can work out the oceans' history.

When the Earth formed, about 4,600 million years ago, it was much too hot to have any water on the surface. As it cooled, water vapor was forced from the rocks within, through volcanoes and cracks, out into the atmosphere. Here it condensed, and the Earth was cloaked in clouds. Eventually it started to rain—and it rained for thousands of years! The waters ran across the rocky landscape, down into vast hollows and basins. Gradually the oceans formed. But all the time, the landmasses were drifting around the globe, so the shapes of the oceans altered. Also the sea levels went up and down with changes in climate, which also altered the shapes of the land and oceans.

THE CONTINENTAL JIGSAW

Evidence for the existence of the super-continent Pangaea comes from the shapes of the continents today. Cut out the continents from a map, and you can fit together these pieces like a jigsaw. For example, the east coast of South America slots into the west coast of Africa. These two places have similar rock layers and similar fossils, giving more evidence.

The best fit
The continents fit together best along the continental shelves, which are the edges of the main landmasses, where the seabed is shallow. The coastlines we see on maps have changed as sea levels go up and down.

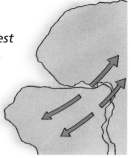

50 million years ago
The Red Sea began to form, as Africa started to drift away from Arabia. The Atlantic Ocean began to widen. Dinosaurs had gone. It was the Age of Mammals.

Humans appeared only about 2.5 million years ago.

The world today—still changing

The Seabed

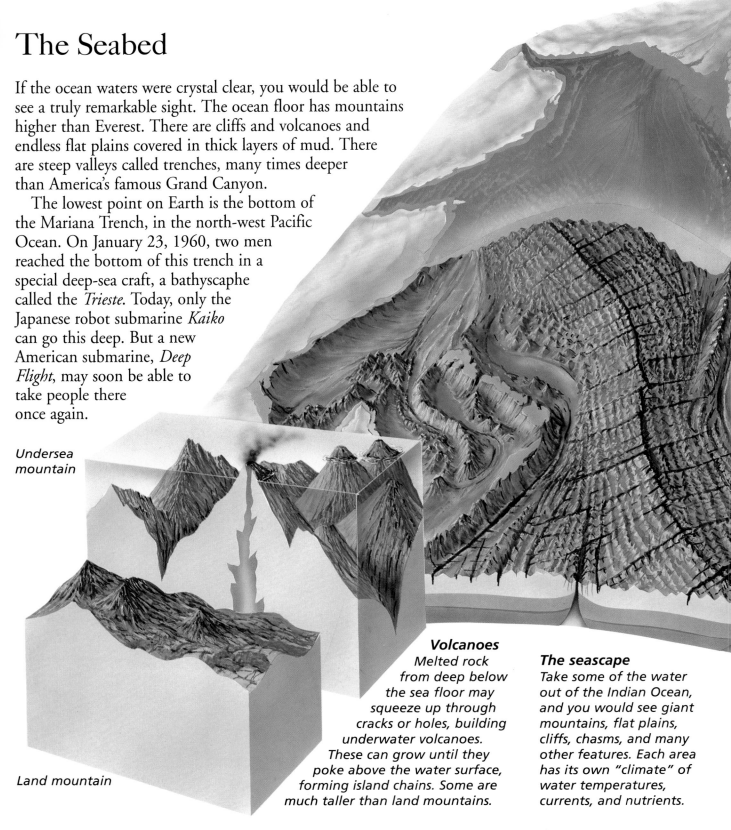

If the ocean waters were crystal clear, you would be able to see a truly remarkable sight. The ocean floor has mountains higher than Everest. There are cliffs and volcanoes and endless flat plains covered in thick layers of mud. There are steep valleys called trenches, many times deeper than America's famous Grand Canyon.

The lowest point on Earth is the bottom of the Mariana Trench, in the north-west Pacific Ocean. On January 23, 1960, two men reached the bottom of this trench in a special deep-sea craft, a bathyscaphe called the *Trieste*. Today, only the Japanese robot submarine *Kaiko* can go this deep. But a new American submarine, *Deep Flight*, may soon be able to take people there once again.

Undersea mountain

Land mountain

Volcanoes
Melted rock from deep below the sea floor may squeeze up through cracks or holes, building underwater volcanoes. These can grow until they poke above the water surface, forming island chains. Some are much taller than land mountains.

The seascape
Take some of the water out of the Indian Ocean, and you would see giant mountains, flat plains, cliffs, chasms, and many other features. Each area has its own "climate" of water temperatures, currents, and nutrients.

20

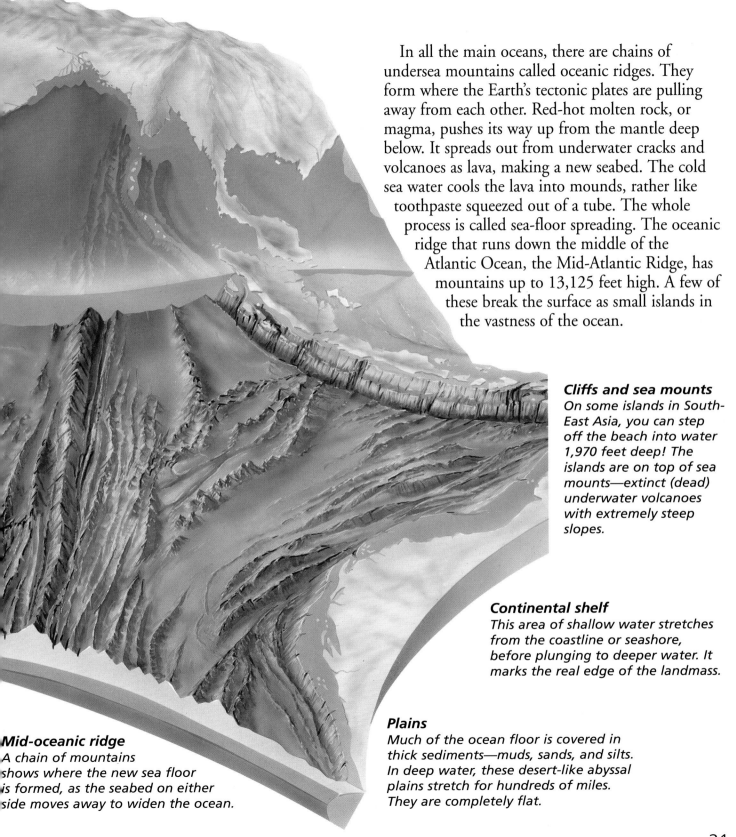

In all the main oceans, there are chains of undersea mountains called oceanic ridges. They form where the Earth's tectonic plates are pulling away from each other. Red-hot molten rock, or magma, pushes its way up from the mantle deep below. It spreads out from underwater cracks and volcanoes as lava, making a new seabed. The cold sea water cools the lava into mounds, rather like toothpaste squeezed out of a tube. The whole process is called sea-floor spreading. The oceanic ridge that runs down the middle of the Atlantic Ocean, the Mid-Atlantic Ridge, has mountains up to 13,125 feet high. A few of these break the surface as small islands in the vastness of the ocean.

Cliffs and sea mounts
On some islands in South-East Asia, you can step off the beach into water 1,970 feet deep! The islands are on top of sea mounts—extinct (dead) underwater volcanoes with extremely steep slopes.

Continental shelf
This area of shallow water stretches from the coastline or seashore, before plunging to deeper water. It marks the real edge of the landmass.

Mid-oceanic ridge
A chain of mountains shows where the new sea floor is formed, as the seabed on either side moves away to widen the ocean.

Plains
Much of the ocean floor is covered in thick sediments—muds, sands, and silts. In deep water, these desert-like abyssal plains stretch for hundreds of miles. They are completely flat.

21

Tides and Shores

The regular up-and-down movements of the sea's surface are called the tides. They are caused by the combined movements of the Earth as it spins around daily on its axis, of the Moon as it goes around the Earth, and of the Earth as it goes around the Sun. The gravities, or pulling effects, of the Moon and the Sun cause the water in the seas and oceans to "bulge" towards them. As the Earth spins, this bulge appears to travel around the world. We see it as the rise and fall of the tide.

On average, there is a time of 12 hours and 25 minutes between one high tide and the next. This means that the high and low tides get later by 50 minutes in every 24-hour day.

Many features affect the height of the tide, such as the size and depth of a sea or ocean, the shape and slope of its coastline, the funnelling effect of narrow straits and estuaries, and wind direction and ocean currents. In the Mediterranean, there is a tidal range—the difference between the highest and lowest water levels—of only about 3 feet. The greatest tidal range is in the Bay of Fundy, north-eastern North America, at 47.5 feet. Spring tides happen when the gravities of Moon and Sun combine.

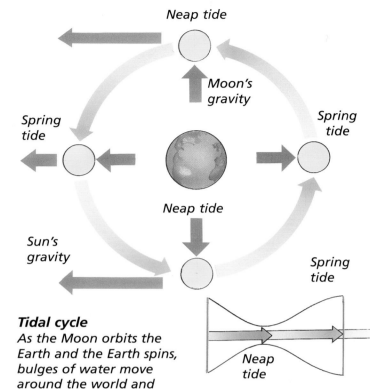

Tidal cycle
As the Moon orbits the Earth and the Earth spins, bulges of water move around the world and create tides. When the Moon and Sun are in line, the extra pull makes spring tides. These happen with the phases of the Moon.

Tidal zones
Spring tides do not just happen in spring. They are the highest high and lowest low ones, as shown on the graph of tidal range, above. Tides are also indicated by bands or zones of wildlife on the shore. The tidal range may be many feet, as shown on the left.

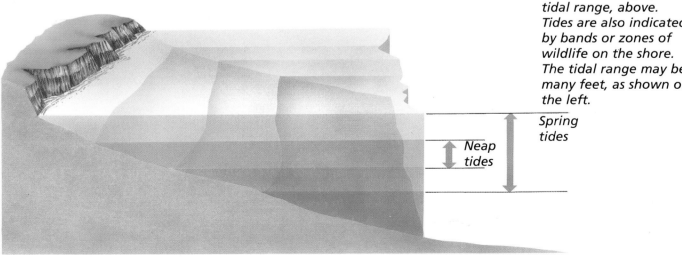

The Power of Water and Ice

Ice can split solid rock, making bits of mountains crack off and erode away. You can demonstrate this safely at home, with the help of an adult.

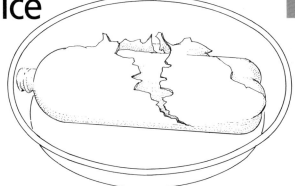

1 Fill a plastic soft-drinks bottle with sink water. Place the cap on tightly. Put the bottle into large bowl (for spillages).

2 Put the bowl into a freezer. Check it quickly every hour, to see what happens. Draw and write down the results.

3 See how as water gets colder and freezes into ice, it also gets bigger or expands. It splits the plastic easily. It can do the same to rocks, stones and metal or plastic plumbing pipes.

4 Repeat the test using water with lots of salt stirred into it, to make a strong salt solution, like sea water. Does it freeze as fast as the clean, fresh water?

Understanding Tides

Twice in every 24 hours, the sea floods over the shore as the tide comes in, and then drains away. The amount of shore uncovered at low tide depends on where you are in the world and how steep the shore is.

Tides are caused mainly by the Moon's gravity, which pulls the water towards it. When the Moon lies over an ocean, it pulls the water up towards itself. As the Earth spins and the Moon circles the Earth, the tides go around too.

1 Use a container of "Slime" from a toy shop. Put the "Slime" on the lid of the pot or on a small saucer and spread it out so it covers the whole surface. The "tide" is in.

2 Use your fingers like the Moon—to pull the slime up towards the middle. As you pull and it piles up, it comes away from the edges. The "tide" is out.

Tide tables
Scientists can predict (work out) the times of high tides and low tides. You can buy small booklets of local tide tables for most seaside resorts. Look for the very high spring tides and much lower neap tides.

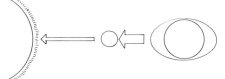

When the Moon and Sun are in line, their gravities add together. The high tide is extra-high and the low tide is extra-low. These are spring tides.

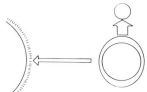

When the Moon and Sun are at right angles, their gravities partly cancel out. The high tide is not very high at all, and the low tide is not at all low. These are neap tides.

Sea against Land

There are many types of shorelines around the world, from high, sheer sea cliffs to squelchy mud-flats that stretch to the horizon. Coasts are shaped by waves, wind, weather, tides, and currents, over thousands and millions of years. Caught up in each wave are bits of sand, pebbles, and rocks. As the waves crash on to the shore, these particles are flung against the land and gradually wear it away. Softer rocks, like sandstone, wear away faster than hard ones, like granite. The endless battering and crashing creates strange rock shapes such as pillars, arches, blowholes, and steps.

The endless battle
Coastlines are fantastic examples of the way our world changes, and show the power of water, wind, and waves. In twenty years' time, this stretch of seaside might look completely different.

Very hard rock has not been worn away, forming an isolated headland.

Recent cliff-fall on to the foreshore will soon be broken up by the waves.

Replanted salt marshes and rebuilt sand dunes protect coast from waves and flood tides.

Recurved sea wall reflects damaging waves back out to sea.

INTO THE SEA

On the east coasts of England and parts of North America, houses fall into the sea each year, as the soft cliffs crumble. Many years ago, these houses were far away from the shore, but the sea has gradually eaten into the land.

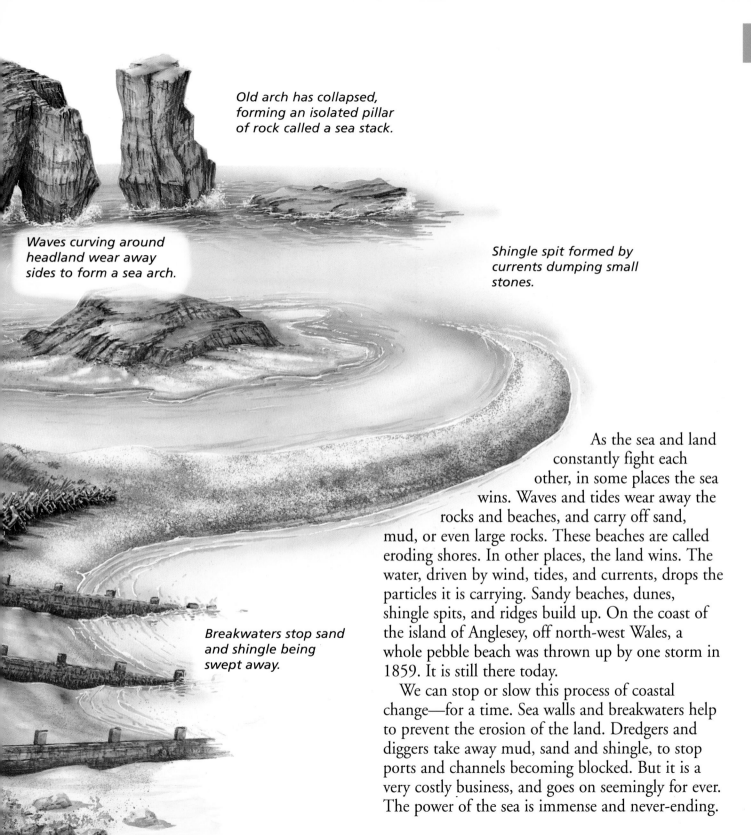

Old arch has collapsed, forming an isolated pillar of rock called a sea stack.

Waves curving around headland wear away sides to form a sea arch.

Shingle spit formed by currents dumping small stones.

Breakwaters stop sand and shingle being swept away.

As the sea and land constantly fight each other, in some places the sea wins. Waves and tides wear away the rocks and beaches, and carry off sand, mud, or even large rocks. These beaches are called eroding shores. In other places, the land wins. The water, driven by wind, tides, and currents, drops the particles it is carrying. Sandy beaches, dunes, shingle spits, and ridges build up. On the coast of the island of Anglesey, off north-west Wales, a whole pebble beach was thrown up by one storm in 1859. It is still there today.

We can stop or slow this process of coastal change—for a time. Sea walls and breakwaters help to prevent the erosion of the land. Dredgers and diggers take away mud, sand and shingle, to stop ports and channels becoming blocked. But it is a very costly business, and goes on seemingly for ever. The power of the sea is immense and never-ending.

Water and Weather

Seas, lakes, and large rivers affect our climate in many different ways. Near the coast, the sea keeps air temperatures fairly even. These places have a maritime climate. If you live by the sea or go on holiday there, you can measure temperature changes in the air and the sea. You could compare them with a place far inland. You can also try this in a lake, pond, or river. Ask an adult to help you take the water temperatures.

Air Temperature

1 To measure air temperature, you need a special shaded place to protect your thermometer from direct sunlight. Make a tube by cutting both ends off a plastic bottle. Paint the outside with white emulsion paint.

2 Tape the tube horizontally across the top of a post about 5 feet high. Tie this to a convenient fence post or to your own post knocked into the ground. It must be out in the open, away from shady buildings or trees.

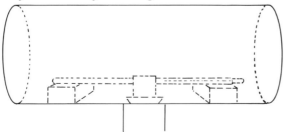

3 Place a standard 0–212°F thermometer or a greenhouse thermometer inside the tube, balanced on two small blocks of wood. Measure the air temperature at the same times each day, such as 8:00 a.m. and 6:00 p.m.

Water Temperature

4 For the sea (or lake) temperature, find a safe place such as a jetty or pontoon. If you are in a harbor, choose the side open to the sea. Lower a bucket down on a rope and fill it up with water. Raise it, dip your thermometer in, and take the temperature.

5 Measure the water temperature at the same times each day, such as 8:00 a.m. and 6:00 p.m. Write the air and water temperatures down in a notebook, with the dates and times.

6 Repeat steps 4 and 5 for a local river or lake, if you can. For instance, if you live next to the sea and you have a friend who lives inland, you could both take your measurements at the same time.

- *Work out which place has the bigger range in air temperature through the day. Is it at the seaside or inland?*
- *Which place has the larger range in water temperature, a river, or the sea? By taking regular weekly or monthly temperatures, you can find out if there are differences between them through the seasons.*
- *Which stays warmest in winter: the sea, a river, or the air?*

From Sea to Land and Back

Life began in the seas, and shores have been "hotbeds of evolution" through the ages. Several times over millions of years, plants and animals have changed and adapted from living in the oceans to coping with the fresh water of rivers and lakes, and even to invading the land and breathing air. Some types of animals, such as whales, have returned again from land back to life in the water.

From the sea
Freshwater fish came out on to land and evolved into amphibians, which then evolved into reptiles. Some reptiles, like crocodiles, went back to the water.

To the sea
Some reptiles grew feathers and took to the air, as birds. Others sprouted fur and evolved into mammals. Members of both groups have gone back to living in water.

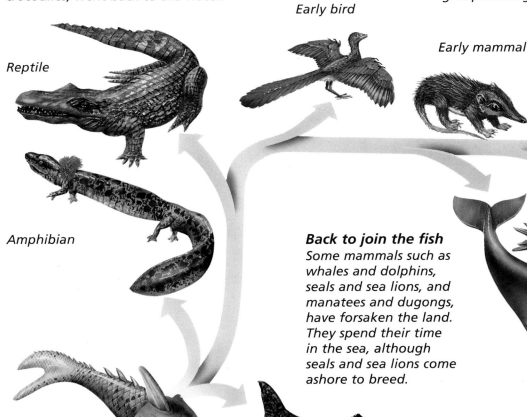

Early bird

Early mammal

Early human

Reptile

Amphibian

Back to join the fish
Some mammals such as whales and dolphins, seals and sea lions, and manatees and dugongs, have forsaken the land. They spend their time in the sea, although seals and sea lions come ashore to breed.

Early fish

Modern freshwater fish

The seas today
Mammals such as dolphins, and also reptiles like sea snakes, are perfectly adapted to marine life.

The Life of a River

There were many legends about the source, or beginning, of a great river. The water there could cure illness, and washed over sparkling gold, jewels, and gems. During the Age of Discovery, explorers made long journeys by boat and foot, to find the sources of great rivers. Often the source turned out to be not very exciting!

Most rivers start as small streams up in the hills, running from a marshy area. A few rivers begin at underground springs. The Ganges in India rises in an ice cave in the Himalaya Mountains. In a very long river like the Nile, it can take six weeks for water to flow from the source to its estuary, or mouth, that opens into the sea.

Source high in mountains

Oxbow lake

The river ends
The estuary may be marked by flat areas of mud or silt, with small branches of the river trickling across them. This is a river delta.

Delta

Mature river
Near the sea, in its lower reaches, the river is older and mature. It meanders or curves across flatter ground. Swamps and marshes are common, and the banks are often flat and very muddy. Many of the world's biggest towns and cities are built along these parts of rivers.

28

Young river

In its young stages, in the mountains or steep hills, a young river is cold, clear, and rushing. It is often a harsh place to live, with strong currents, cold water, and a scoured rocky floor. It may cut a steep-sided gorge into the rocks.

Waterfall

Gorge

As a river journeys to the sea, it changes its character and grows older, from youth to maturity. In its young stages it is often a clear, fast-flowing stream, rushing down steep slopes, high in the hills. The current is very fast, and the water does not contain much food, so few plants or animals can survive. Gradually the slope becomes less, and the river widens as it is joined by tributaries. There may be rapids, waterfalls, lakes, sandbars, islands, or even an underground section. These depend on the rocks that lie under the landscape, how hard they are and how fast they wear away, and if they are porous or "spongy," and are able to soak up the water.

Middle-aged river

The river runs more slowly. Many smaller streams and rivers (tributaries) join, and it becomes wider and perhaps deeper. The river bed is more varied, with stony areas and muddy patches. More plants grow in the mud and weaker currents. They provide homes and food for numerous birds, insects, and other animals.

Today, many rivers do not "grow old" naturally. We change them by building dams across them, and by taking water from them for farms, homes, and industry. The River Volga in Russia now has so many dams that its famous fish, sturgeon and salmon, can no longer swim back up the river to lay their eggs. The once-mighty Colorado River in North America, which cut the Grand Canyon, ends in a trickle in Mexico. Much of its water is channelled away to grow fruit and flowers in the formerly dry scrub and deserts of California. The spectacular Niagara Falls, 164 feet high, are on the Niagara River, on the border between Canada and the USA. But they have only two-thirds of the water that once roared over them. The rest is diverted for hydroelectric power.

Sick Rivers

Fresh, clean water is one of our most precious resources. We cannot survive without it. Apart from drinking it, we use water from rivers and lakes to water our crops, wash ourselves and clothes and other things, to provide electrical power, manufacture goods, carry away sewage and waste, get from place to place, and enjoy ourselves. As a result, there is hardly a river in the world that has not been changed by human activities.

River plants come in all shapes and sizes. Giant Amazon water lily leaves are so big, you could sit on one without sinking! The tiny water plants called algae may be visible only with a microscope. But plants of all kinds are the basis of life in our rivers. They feed plant-eating animals, who are hunted in turn by predatory river animals. Reed beds give shelter to nesting birds, frogs, and other amphibians, and to young water mammals like water rats and beavers. Few plants live in the flowing water, but they thrive along the banks. This is why bank clearance—for boat moorings, fishing platforms, a factory, or power station—has such a devastating effect on river life.

Pesticides and fertilizers wash from the land into the river and pollute the water.

Riverside plants help to keep the water clean and provide food and shelter for animals.

Clear felling of a forest can cause massive erosion and serious pollution of a river.

Wastes pour into the river from factory outfall pipes.

Few plants and animals survive in this polluted water.

Ships dump wastes, used oil, and fuels.

There are also changes in the water which we cannot see, but which greatly affect the river and its wildlife. Polluting chemicals pour in from factories and waste treatment plants. As rain trickles through the soil of farmland into rivers, it collects chemicals such as pesticides and fertilizers. These upset the balance of

nutrients in the water. Some lakes and rivers may suddenly change color. Tiny colored algae float in the water, and they sometimes grow so fast that they turn the water into a soup which seems to be stained red, green, or brown. These algal "blooms" happen when the water has high levels of plant foods, especially minerals such as phosphates and nitrates, from sewage or farmland fertilizer. It is a case of too much food being bad. The algae flourish for a few days or weeks, use up all the oxygen, die and rot, and produce poisons. Fish and other wildlife suffer. The same thing can happen in the sea near the coast. Then it is called a red tide.

Good and bad
With careful planning and management, rivers can provide both for us and for wildlife. But some schemes spell disaster for the natural life of the river. If plants cannot grow along the banks, river animals have no food or shelter, and wildlife disappears.

Water is taken from the river for drinking, washing, crops, and industry.

Strong sunlight

Algal blooms
In water super-rich with nutrients, algae flourish and then perish, poisoned by their own wastes. As they rot, they suffocate other river life.

Well-treated sewage soon disperses and has no lasting effects.

Excessive nutrients in water

Algae rot and water putrefies

A straightened, canalized river with steep, bare sides cannot support bank plants.

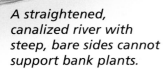

PLANTS GONE WILD

Sometimes, water plants are taken to a new area, where they have no natural checks on their growth, and no animals to eat them. They go wild and grow fast. In the 1970s, animals in Australia's Lake Moondarra were suffocating. The water was completely covered by a fern, introduced accidentally from Brazil. Eventually scientists solved the problem by introducing a beetle that liked to eat the fern. Water hyacinth (left) has clogged vast areas of rivers and lakes around the world, and is the number-one water-weed pest.

Winter and Summer

Redpoll

Heron

In the depths of winter, when water on land is frozen, animals come to the river to drink.

Fox

Snowdrops

Water rail

Water vol

Places such as Europe and North America have cold winters and warm summers. They are called temperate lands. As winter approaches, the river and its wildlife change. Trees lose their leaves. Grasses, reeds, rushes, and other bank plants stop growing and die back, so the banks look bare. Many birds fly away to warmer countries. Some small animals, such as insects, die off, but first they lay eggs, which may develop into larvae or pupae. These can survive the cold and frost. These insects, along with worms, snails, and myriad other small creatures, survive winter buried in the cold mud on the river bed. Bank creatures sleep in their nests. Fish save energy by lying still, on or in the mud. Water temperature falls. Life almost comes to a halt.

As spring approaches, life begins to stir again. The longer hours of daylight and rising temperatures encourage plant growth. Melting ice

Grayling

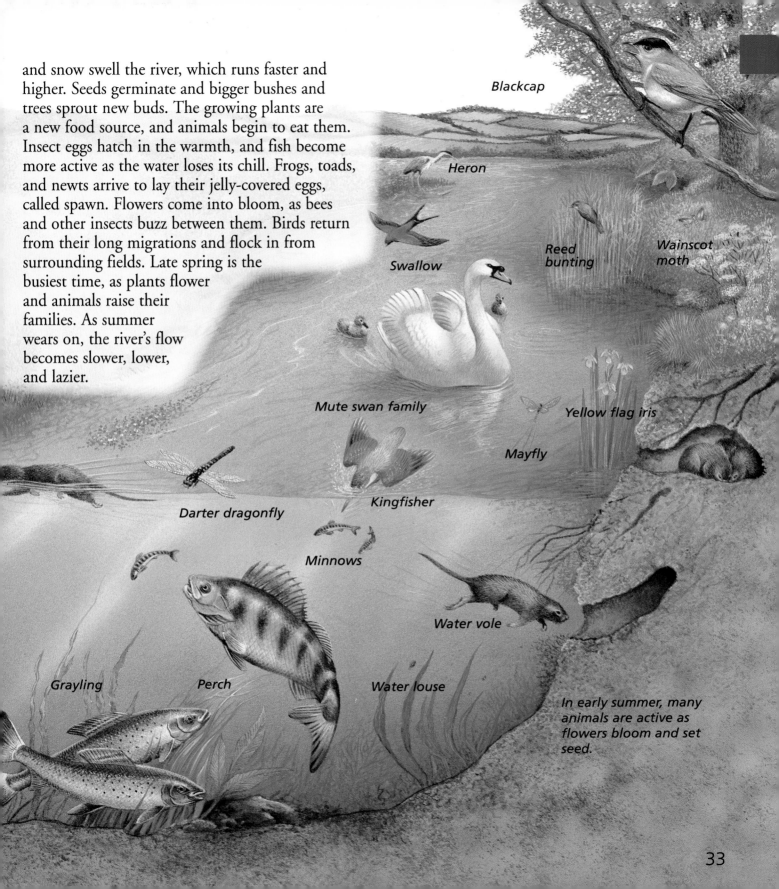

and snow swell the river, which runs faster and higher. Seeds germinate and bigger bushes and trees sprout new buds. The growing plants are a new food source, and animals begin to eat them. Insect eggs hatch in the warmth, and fish become more active as the water loses its chill. Frogs, toads, and newts arrive to lay their jelly-covered eggs, called spawn. Flowers come into bloom, as bees and other insects buzz between them. Birds return from their long migrations and flock in from surrounding fields. Late spring is the busiest time, as plants flower and animals raise their families. As summer wears on, the river's flow becomes slower, lower, and lazier.

Blackcap

Heron

Swallow

Reed bunting

Wainscot moth

Mute swan family

Yellow flag iris

Mayfly

Darter dragonfly

Kingfisher

Minnows

Water vole

Grayling

Perch

Water louse

In early summer, many animals are active as flowers bloom and set seed.

33

Hunters of the River

The watery jungles of plants found alongside rivers and lakes, and in marshes, mangrove swamps and other wet areas, are very important for wildlife. Flamingoes, river dolphins, beavers, and even tigers live in these wetlands. Some large areas, such as the Camargue in France, the Coto Doñana in Spain and the Everglades of Florida, have been made into National Parks. Unfortunately many have now been drained to prevent flooding, create more farmland and make ports. Over half of the world's wetlands have disappeared in the last fifty years.

The web of life in a river builds up from the plants, to the herbivores, or plant-eating animals. Many of these, such as copepods, water fleas (daphnia) and tiny worms, are so small you can hardly see them. Others are very obvious, from water snails and larger worms to water rats, coypu and river turtles. At the top of the food webs

Otter
This fierce hunter twists and turns with great agility as it swims after fish, crayfish, frogs, large insects, and other prey.

Minnows
These finger-sized members of the carp family swim in large shoals. They are regular victims of many river hunters.

Bream
The bream likes sluggish, muddy rivers, canals, and lakes, where it feeds on tiny items of food on the bottom.

Pike
Often the largest predator in its lake or river, a pike lurks in weeds and dashes out to grab victims in its huge mouth.

are the carnivores, or hunters. They vary across the world, but they usually include large insect larvae, snakes, aquatic (water-dwelling) mammals such as otters and mink, and birds like kingfishers and fish-eagles. The main river predators are fish. They are found almost everywhere, from swift, clear upland streams to the slow, muddy reaches near the sea. Each kind is adapted to a particular zone of the river. When rivers are deepened and straightened to prevent floods, they become less suitable as homes for fish.

Salmon
This fish returns to the river where it hatched, to breed and perhaps die. It may snap at flies or other small food.

Trout
With its small but sharp and numerous teeth, a trout catches a variety of prey, such as worms, insects, and young fish.

Perch
A voracious predator, the perch hunts all manner of smaller fish, such as roach, bleak, and minnows. It lies in wait among water plants.

LIVING EGG-CASE

The bitterling, a small European lake fish, has an amazing way of breeding. The female grows a long tube, through which she lays her eggs in a freshwater mussel. The mussel's hard shell protects the babies as they develop.

35

Life in the Swamps

A forest of trees sticking up out of the water is usually a sign of a flood. But some forests grow in water. They are forests of mangrove and cypress trees. Some types of mangroves grow in salty water, along the sheltered, muddy, tidal shores of tropical seas. They also grow along the banks and swamps of river estuaries, up to 60 miles inland. It is difficult to walk through a mangrove forest, even when the tide is out. This is because some of their roots grow up into the air, instead of down! Also the mud is thick, sticky and deep. There is very little oxygen in such waterlogged ground, and the aerial roots take in air and help the trees to breathe.

Like rainforests, mangrove forests and swamps are disappearing. Some have been cut down to provide timber, since mangrove wood has many uses, such as in building houses, as pilings for piers and wharfs, and as firewood. Other mangrove areas are cleared to make space for fish-farming ponds, or for ports, oil refineries, power stations and factories.

Scarlet ibis
This bright bird from coastal South America lives and breeds on mudflats, estuaries, and mangrove swamps.

The top hunter
The largest and most fearsome predator is the estuarine or saltwater crocodile. But it has become very rare, and is now protected as an endangered species.

Forest on the seashore
Mangrove forests are very rich in wildlife. Monkeys, birds, reptiles and many insects live there. Crabs, mudskippers, and worms crawl in the mud. Fish such as stingrays, as well as prawns and shrimps, swim between the roots when the tide is in.

Grazing the weeds
Sea cows such as manatees and dugongs are large aquatic mammals. They graze the water plants, as cows graze grass on land.

Shooting prey
The archer fish may venture from the river to the estuary, to spit at prey above.

However, mangrove forests stop mud and sand from being swept away by the waves. So, if they are cut down, the sea sometimes floods inland during storms. Nearby coral reefs may be killed as the mud is washed along the coast and settles on the corals, choking and suffocating them. Conservationists are worried by the amount of forest being cleared. In Ecuador, South America, one-third of all the mangroves were cut down between 1979 and 1983.

Cypress trees also form freshwater forests, as in the Everglades in Florida. They are home to manatees (sea cows), alligators, the very rare Florida panther, pelicans, and 300 other kinds of birds. But some of these important wildlife areas are being polluted with chemicals, or drying out as water is pumped away to nearby towns. The number of wading birds in the Everglades has dropped by more than nine-tenths in the last 125 years.

Skipping across the mud
Mudskippers have large gill chambers on the side of the head, to hold water. So they can stay in the air for many minutes, skipping over the mud on their strong fins.

Aerial roots help to take in oxygen so the trees do not suffocate in the mud.

Prop roots help to hold the trees upright in the soft mud.

Keep off my patch!
As the tide goes out, fiddler crabs emerge from their burrows. Each has a patch of mud where it feeds. It guards this territory fiercely, waving its huge claw as a warning to rivals to keep away.

The River Through the Year

You can build up a valuable picture of a local river and see how it changes through the year, using a combination of maps, sketches, pictures and samples. You may be able to get help from a local wildlife or nature group. Always go with others on this sort of expedition (see the advice in the front of this book).

You will need a sturdy net with a long handle, a plastic box or bucket for your catch, a notebook and pencil, local maps, old wildlife magazines, and a long, large piece of paper such as leftover wallpaper.

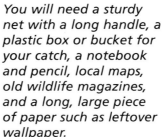

1 Plan to visit the river in late spring or summer and in the middle of winter. If you have a camera, take photographs of your site. Make sure you include plants growing on the bank and in the water.

2 In your notebook, write down where you stood to take the photos. On your following visits, try to take photos from exactly the same spot. Compare the winter and summer pictures.

3 On each visit, use your dip net to catch as many river animals as you can. Use the net in different places such as underneath water weeds, along the water surface, and down in the mud.

4 Look at your catch in a water-filled plastic box, bucket, or white tray. Write down all the animals you have found. Use books to help you identify them. If you can't recognize an animal, make a sketch of it in your notebook.

5 From a proper map, draw a large sketch map of the river along the paper. Add features such as bridges and islands. Stick on photos cut out of old magazines of the animals and plants you see, or draw pictures of them.

6 You could measure the river's water temperature (see page 26) and the level of the water, and estimate its speed (current). You might make two such maps, for summer and winter visits. Are there many differences?

At the Edge of the Sea

Seaweeds can make a visit to a rocky seashore a very slippery experience! They belong to the group of plants called algae, which do not have proper roots, stems, or flowers. Their "leaves" are called fronds, the "stems" are stipes, and the "roots" are holdfasts. Most seaweeds flop over on the rocks when the tide is out. When the tide comes in, the water holds them up. This water provides minerals and nutrients, and the holdfast simply attaches the seaweed tightly to the rocks or seabed.

Like land plants, seaweeds need light to grow, so they can only live on the shore or in shallow water. The clearer the water, the deeper they live. Where coastal waters are murky, especially where rivers enter the sea, there are no seaweeds. Most tropical shores are too hot for seaweeds to grow well.

Living in layers
Seaweeds grow in bands or zones along the shore, determined by the up and down movements of the tide, and by exposure to wind and waves. Brown wracks and kelps cover many rocky shores in northern Europe and North America.

Average high-tide mark

Lichen-covered rocks of splash zone

Red seaweeds
Most cannot survive any dryness, so they grow low on the shore, in the shade of larger weeds or in deeper water.

Bladder wrack
The air-filled bladders keep the fronds floating up near the light.

Average low-tide mark

Cuvie (forest kelp)
The broad fronds, shaped like palm leaves, are very tough and leathery.

Sublittoral zone (always submerged)

Sea lettuce
This thin, delicate weed has a very small holdfast and its thin, delicate fronds easily break free.

Furbelows
This kelp has a bulging holdfast covered with pimples.

39

Forests of the Shallows

Where on Earth could you find an untouched forest, teeming with colorful animals and plants, right next to a busy city? Stand on a beach in San Francisco, California, and look out just beyond the breaking waves. There, hidden beneath the sea's surface, are great underwater forests swaying in rhythm with the waves. The forest's "trees" are large, brown seaweeds called kelps. Giant kelp is the largest water plant in the world. It can grow by more than an arm's length each day. Fully grown, it stretches more than 200 feet. Kelp forests grow only in well-lit, cool waters below about 68°F.

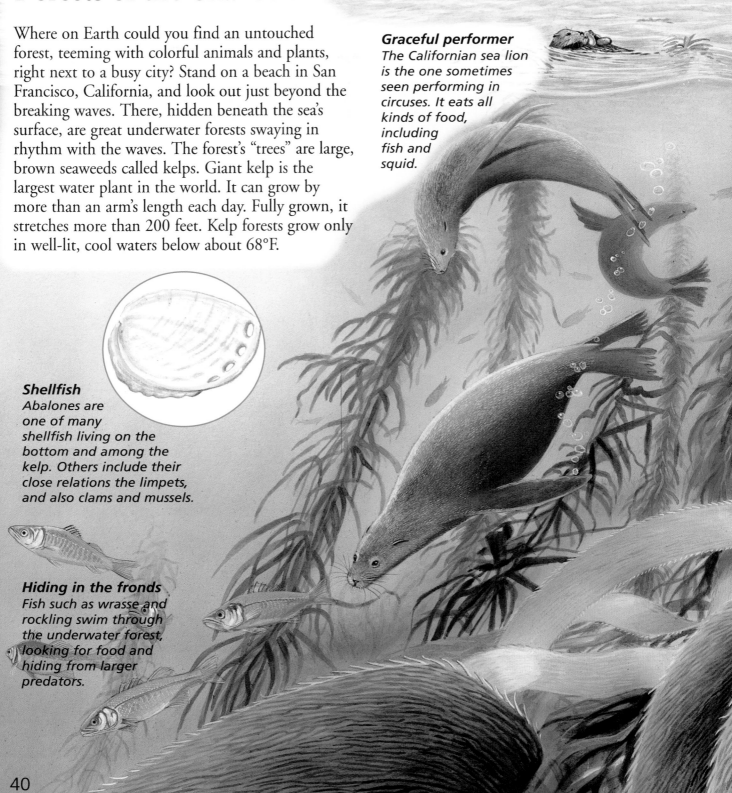

Graceful performer
The Californian sea lion is the one sometimes seen performing in circuses. It eats all kinds of food, including fish and squid.

Shellfish
Abalones are one of many shellfish living on the bottom and among the kelp. Others include their close relations the limpets, and also clams and mussels.

Hiding in the fronds
Fish such as wrasse and rockling swim through the underwater forest, looking for food and hiding from larger predators.

Giant kelp forests grow along the Pacific coast of America near Chile and Peru. Other kelp forests, including the types named oarweeds, are found in northern Europe, southern Australia, New Zealand, South Africa and islands near Antarctica.

These vast underwater habitats provide homes, food and hunting grounds for a great variety of fish, snails, crabs, and larger animals including seals, dolphins, and otters. One of the commonest animals is the prickly sea urchin, which chews up the seaweeds and the small animals attached to them. Recently, some Californian kelp forests have been destroyed by armies of sea urchins. Their numbers are usually kept down by predators such as sea otters and sheepshead fish. Unfortunately these have become scarce due to human activities, so urchin numbers have grown.

The shellfish hammer
The sea otter is one of the few tool-using animals. With a rock from the sea bed, it smashes open its food of abalones, other shellfish, and sea urchins.

Autumn fronds
Like tree leaves, the fronds of kelp are shed once or twice a year. Small balloons of gas, known as bladders, help to keep them upright so they can get sufficient light.

The Slow-motion Jungle

What is the difference between an animal and a plant? Is it that plants stay rooted to the spot and make their own food with the help of sunlight, while animals move around and eat plants or other animals? This is mostly true on land, but not in the sea! Many marine animals look and behave like plants. They stay firmly fixed to rocks or "rooted" in sand and mud.

On land, animals stuck in one place would probably starve. But in the sea, food is brought to them. Water currents carry the tiny floating animals and plants of the plankton. Animals like sponges and sea squirts suck the water in, filter the food from it and squirt the waste water out again. Other fixed creatures, like anemones, tube-worms, and sea fans, actively catch their food with their waving, sticky tentacles. Barnacles use their feathery feet to kick tiny bits of food into their mouths!

Filtering the sea
Mussels, oysters, scallops, and clams belong to the mollusk group. Their two shell halves, called valves, gape slightly so they can take in water and filter food from it.

Pipe fish
This long-nosed fish sucks in tiny particles of food through its tube-shaped mouth. It usually hides among plants such as eel grass, gripping with its curly tail.

Oarweed

Plumose anemone

Tube-worm

Lobster

Flowery animal
The sea anemone is an upside-down relative of the jellyfish. Its tentacles grasp and sting prey, and push it into the stomach in the hollow stalk.

Sponge

Mussels

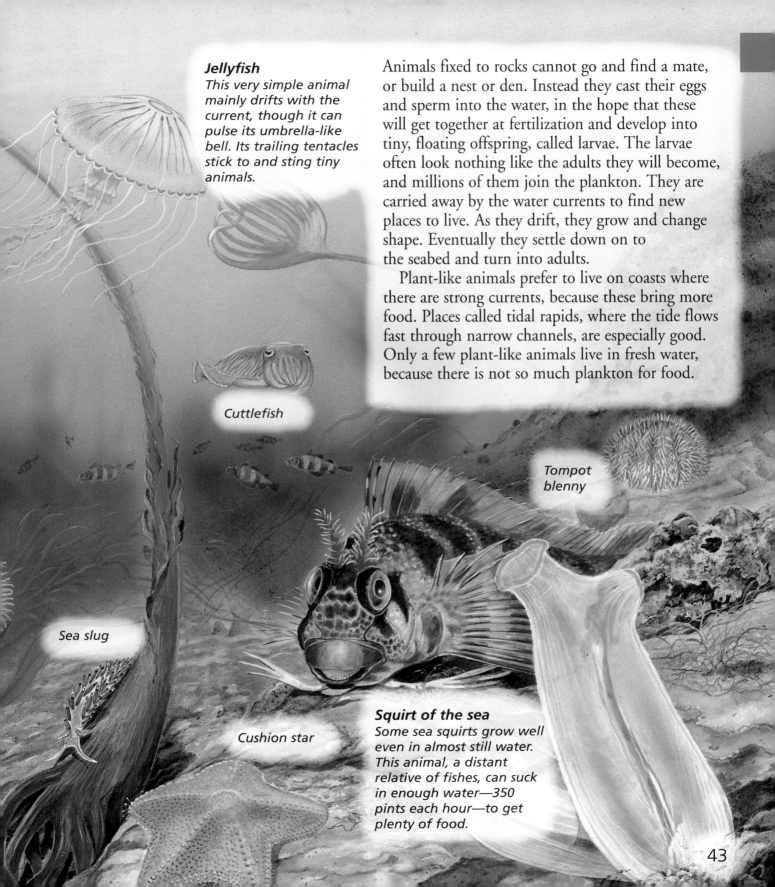

Jellyfish
This very simple animal mainly drifts with the current, though it can pulse its umbrella-like bell. Its trailing tentacles stick to and sting tiny animals.

Animals fixed to rocks cannot go and find a mate, or build a nest or den. Instead they cast their eggs and sperm into the water, in the hope that these will get together at fertilization and develop into tiny, floating offspring, called larvae. The larvae often look nothing like the adults they will become, and millions of them join the plankton. They are carried away by the water currents to find new places to live. As they drift, they grow and change shape. Eventually they settle down on to the seabed and turn into adults.

Plant-like animals prefer to live on coasts where there are strong currents, because these bring more food. Places called tidal rapids, where the tide flows fast through narrow channels, are especially good. Only a few plant-like animals live in fresh water, because there is not so much plankton for food.

Cuttlefish

Tompot blenny

Sea slug

Cushion star

Squirt of the sea
Some sea squirts grow well even in almost still water. This animal, a distant relative of fishes, can suck in enough water—350 pints each hour—to get plenty of food.

43

Buried Alive!

Sandy beaches are lovely places to walk and play. They are also home for many buried animals. For example, lugworms live in U-shaped burrows about 8–12 inches deep, marked by squiggly piles of sand called worm casts. Buried shellfish such as clams have two long, fleshy tubes called siphons, that stretch to the surface. One tube sucks down water containing food and oxygen, which is filtered and absorbed by the animal. The unwanted water is squirted back up the other tube. Some shellfish have extra-long siphons that they poke above the surface and wave about like miniature vacuum cleaners, sucking in food. Heart urchins, sand dollars, and ragworms move slowly through the sand searching for food.

Try to walk along the black, muddy shores of an estuary and you would soon get stuck! The smelly, sticky mud may seem unpleasant to us. But it is full of nutrients and supports incredible numbers of buried creatures, especially worms and shellfish. Cockles, oysters, clams, and other shellfish are grown in sheltered estuaries all over the world, as food for people. If the water is polluted, the shellfish can collect poisons in their bodies. Fish, birds and people eating them can be ill or even die.

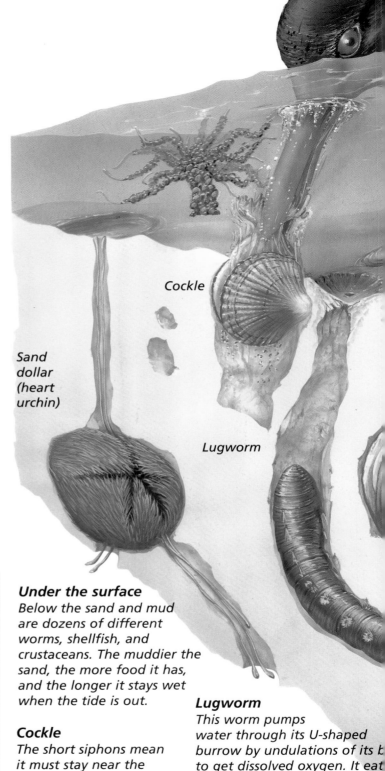

Cockle

Sand dollar (heart urchin)

Lugworm

SIGNS ON THE SURFACE

As the lugworm sucks down water and sand, a small saucer-shaped hole forms above it on the surface. The worm eats the sand, digests any bits of food, and ejects the leftovers from its tail, to form a squiggly worm cast on the surface.

Under the surface
Below the sand and mud are dozens of different worms, shellfish, and crustaceans. The muddier the sand, the more food it has, and the longer it stays wet when the tide is out.

Cockle
The short siphons mean it must stay near the surface, where it is easy prey for birds and fish.

Lugworm
This worm pumps water through its U-shaped burrow by undulations of its b to get dissolved oxygen. It eat the sand and digests nutrients just like an earthworm in soil.

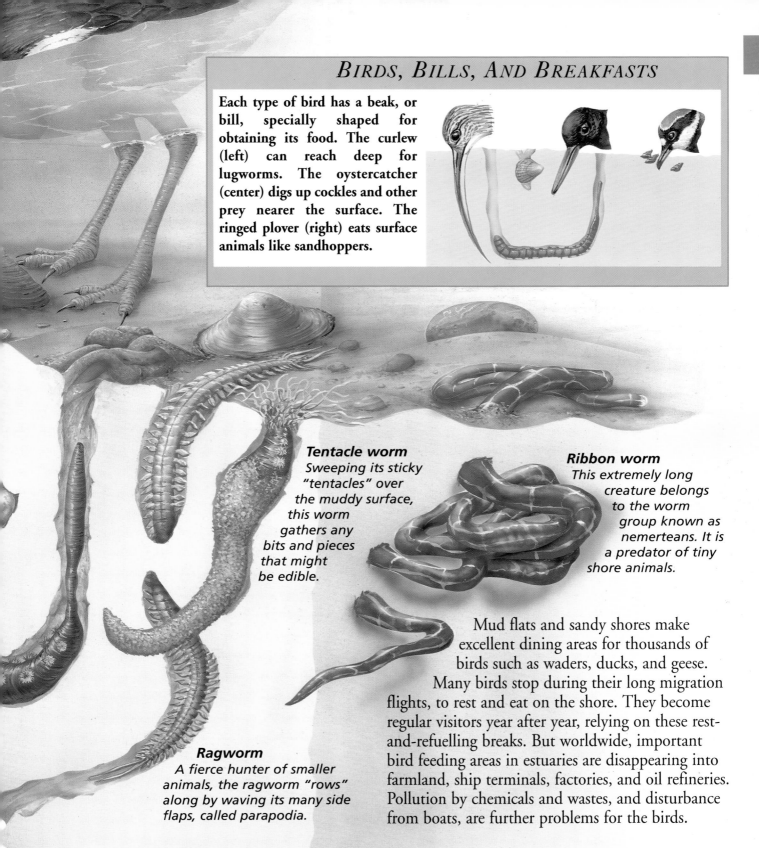

BIRDS, BILLS, AND BREAKFASTS

Each type of bird has a beak, or bill, specially shaped for obtaining its food. The curlew (left) can reach deep for lugworms. The oystercatcher (center) digs up cockles and other prey nearer the surface. The ringed plover (right) eats surface animals like sandhoppers.

Tentacle worm
Sweeping its sticky "tentacles" over the muddy surface, this worm gathers any bits and pieces that might be edible.

Ribbon worm
This extremely long creature belongs to the worm group known as nemerteans. It is a predator of tiny shore animals.

Ragworm
A fierce hunter of smaller animals, the ragworm "rows" along by waving its many side flaps, called parapodia.

Mud flats and sandy shores make excellent dining areas for thousands of birds such as waders, ducks, and geese. Many birds stop during their long migration flights, to rest and eat on the shore. They become regular visitors year after year, relying on these rest-and-refuelling breaks. But worldwide, important bird feeding areas in estuaries are disappearing into farmland, ship terminals, factories, and oil refineries. Pollution by chemicals and wastes, and disturbance from boats, are further problems for the birds.

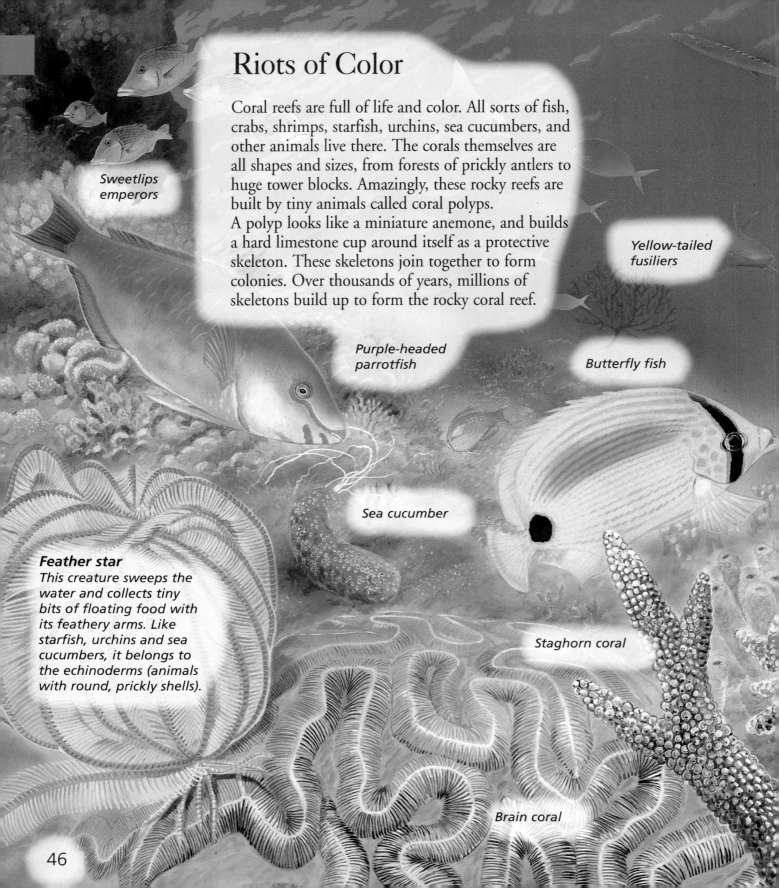

Riots of Color

Coral reefs are full of life and color. All sorts of fish, crabs, shrimps, starfish, urchins, sea cucumbers, and other animals live there. The corals themselves are all shapes and sizes, from forests of prickly antlers to huge tower blocks. Amazingly, these rocky reefs are built by tiny animals called coral polyps.

A polyp looks like a miniature anemone, and builds a hard limestone cup around itself as a protective skeleton. These skeletons join together to form colonies. Over thousands of years, millions of skeletons build up to form the rocky coral reef.

Sweetlips emperors

Yellow-tailed fusiliers

Purple-headed parrotfish

Butterfly fish

Sea cucumber

Feather star
This creature sweeps the water and collects tiny bits of floating food with its feathery arms. Like starfish, urchins and sea cucumbers, it belongs to the echinoderms (animals with round, prickly shells).

Staghorn coral

Brain coral

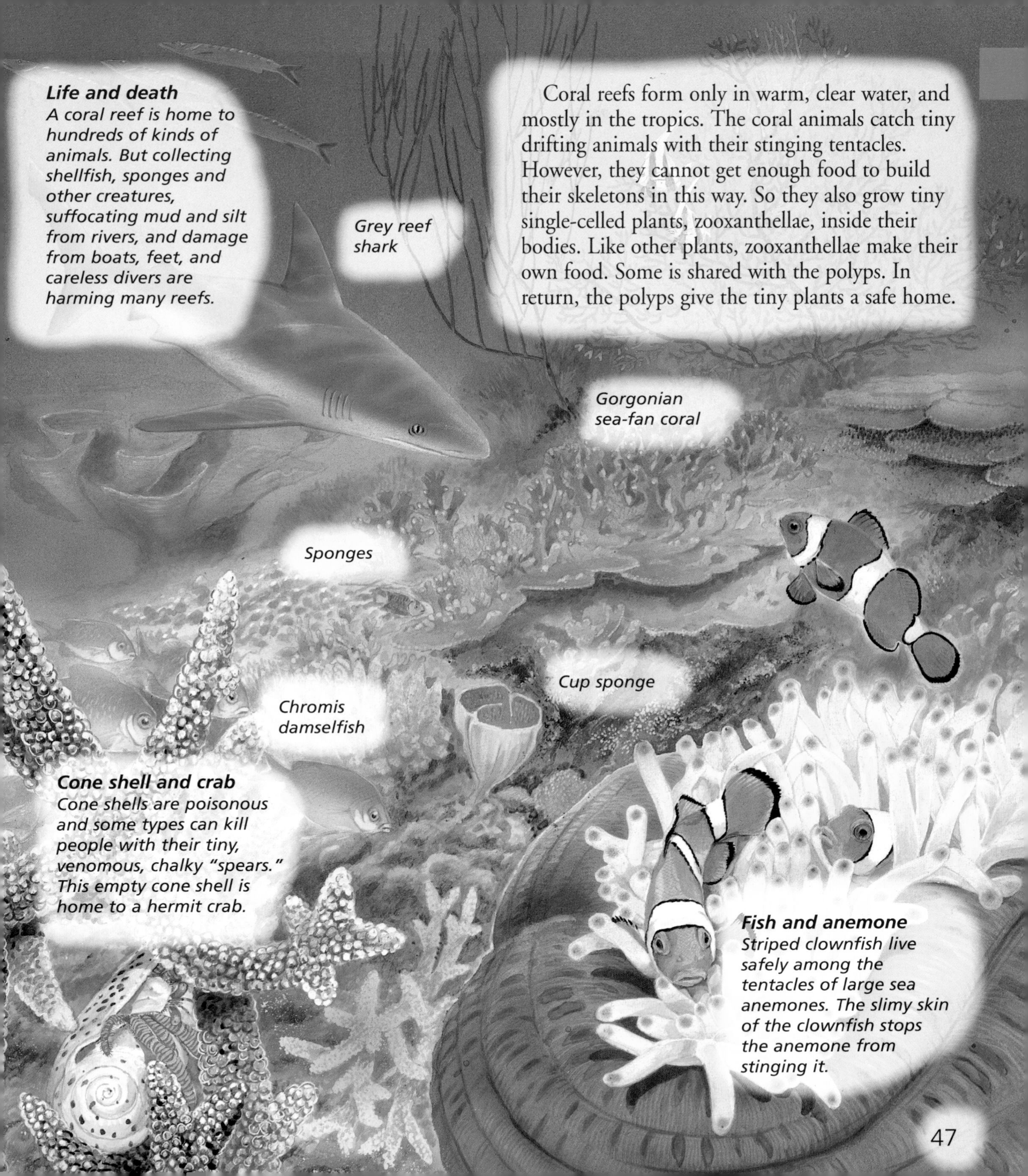

Life and death
A coral reef is home to hundreds of kinds of animals. But collecting shellfish, sponges and other creatures, suffocating mud and silt from rivers, and damage from boats, feet, and careless divers are harming many reefs.

Coral reefs form only in warm, clear water, and mostly in the tropics. The coral animals catch tiny drifting animals with their stinging tentacles. However, they cannot get enough food to build their skeletons in this way. So they also grow tiny single-celled plants, zooxanthellae, inside their bodies. Like other plants, zooxanthellae make their own food. Some is shared with the polyps. In return, the polyps give the tiny plants a safe home.

Grey reef shark

Gorgonian sea-fan coral

Sponges

Cup sponge

Chromis damselfish

Cone shell and crab
Cone shells are poisonous and some types can kill people with their tiny, venomous, chalky "spears." This empty cone shell is home to a hermit crab.

Fish and anemone
Striped clownfish live safely among the tentacles of large sea anemones. The slimy skin of the clownfish stops the anemone from stinging it.

Clean Water

We depend on fresh, clean, clear water—not only to drink, but also for cooking and washing in the home, and for hundreds of industrial and factory processes. Dirty water carries germs and harmful chemicals. In Nature, water is cleaned and filtered as it trickles through the ground and the rocks, so that water coming from a mountain spring or a well can be very pure. Copy this process and filter dirty water using coffee filter paper, clean sand, fine powdered charcoal (crushed from barbecue charcoal), and a large funnel.

1 Make some dirty water by adding a tablespoon of garden soil to 2 pints of clean tap water in a bowl. Stir this well so that it becomes cloudy and "muddy."

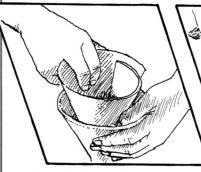

2 Fold the coffee filter paper in half, then into quarters. Then open it slightly into a cone shape that fits snugly into the funnel, and press it in place.

3 Make your filtering layers or beds by putting 2 tablespoons of clean sand in the bottom of the filter cone. Cover with a layer of 3 tablespoons of powdered charcoal.

4 Add a top layer of 4 tablespoons of sand. Put the whole funnel into a tall jug. Now pour the dirty water slowly onto the filter beds, trying not to disturb the layers.

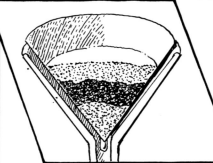

5 The water trickles down through the beds. The sand traps large particles, and the charcoal traps or soaks up smaller ones. The filter paper helps, too.

6 The result is much cleaner water! This is how rain water is filtered naturally, as it trickles through pebbles, sand, and various layers of rocks, in the ground.

WARNING: Do not drink your filtered water. It may contain invisible germs. Proper drinking water from the faucet is filtered much more thoroughly and treated to kill germs, at the water treatment works.

Making Salty Water Fresh

In many hot and dry countries, clean and fresh drinking water is very scarce. One method of obtaining fresh water is to get rid of the salt and other dissolved substances in sea water. This is known as desalination.

You need a clean metal saucepan with its well-fitting clean lid, half a cup of table salt, tap water, a clean mug, effective oven gloves, and a stove. Also, you MUST have adult help with this activity, as stove tops and hot water can be very dangerous.

1 *First, make your own sea water. Put tap water into the saucepan until it is about one-third full. Slowly add the salt, stirring so that it dissolves thoroughly. Take a tiny sip, if you dare. It tastes horrible!*

2 *Now heat your salty "sea water." Ask the adult to set the burner controls so that the water will simmer gently, without boiling. Wait for a few minutes with the lid off, until it warms up and begins to steam slightly.*

3 *Ask the adult to place the lid on the saucepan. After a minute or two, he or she lifts off the lid. On its underside are droplets of water. Hold the lid over the mug and tilt it so that the drops run into the mug.*

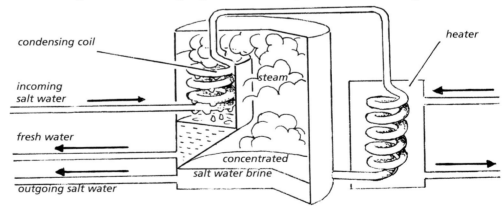

condensing coil

incoming salt water

fresh water

outgoing salt water

steam

heater

concentrated salt water brine

4 *Do this several times, so the mug has about ¹/2 inch of water in it. Turn off the burner and let everything go cool for 15 to 30 minutes. Now sip the water in the mug. No salt! The cool water in the pan may be even saltier!*

The heat from the burner makes the liquid water in the pan evaporate, or turn into water vapor and the tiny droplets which we see as "steam." These rise into the air. But the salt is not affected, and it stays behind in the pan. On the saucepan lid, the steam cools and condenses, or turns back to pure liquid water without anything dissolved in it. A real desalination plant purifies thousands of gallons of water every hour, using heat from the Sun or massive fuel-powered boilers.

The Open Ocean

Life on Earth depends on plants. Without them, animals would have nothing to eat and no oxygen in the air to breathe. On land, we can see plants such as grasses, flowers, and trees. On the seashore, we can see the seaweeds. But in the open ocean, we cannot see the plants. They are there—but they are very small, usually microscopic. They are called plant plankton, or phytoplankton.

These tiny plants belong to the plant group algae, which also includes shore seaweeds. One of the commonest types of algae is the diatoms. They are shaped like tiny pill boxes, rods, pointed hats or chains. There may be millions of diatoms and other microscopic algae in a bucket of sea water, making it into a type of greenish soup. This plant plankton is the "grass and leaves" of the sea—the basic food for all animal life.

The plant plankton is eaten by animal plankton, or zooplankton. This consists of tiny creatures

Big and small
The largest fish in the world is the harmless whale shark, 46 feet long. Yet it feeds by filtering from the water some of the smallest sea creatures—tiny fish, shrimps, and other animal plankton.

Micro-plants
Plant plankton consists of diatoms, dinoflagellates, and other microscopic algae. Some have beautiful cases or shells made of glass-like silica. They need light to grow, so they live mainly in the upper layers of sea water, to about 330 feet depth. They are the basic food for all sea life.

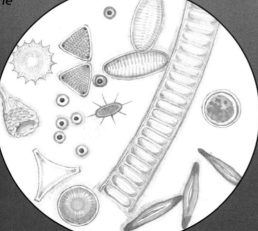

Krill
These finger-sized creatures are related to shrimps and crabs. Billions of them swarm in cooler seas, especially around Antarctica. They are eaten by whales, penguins, squid, seals, and many larger sea creatures.

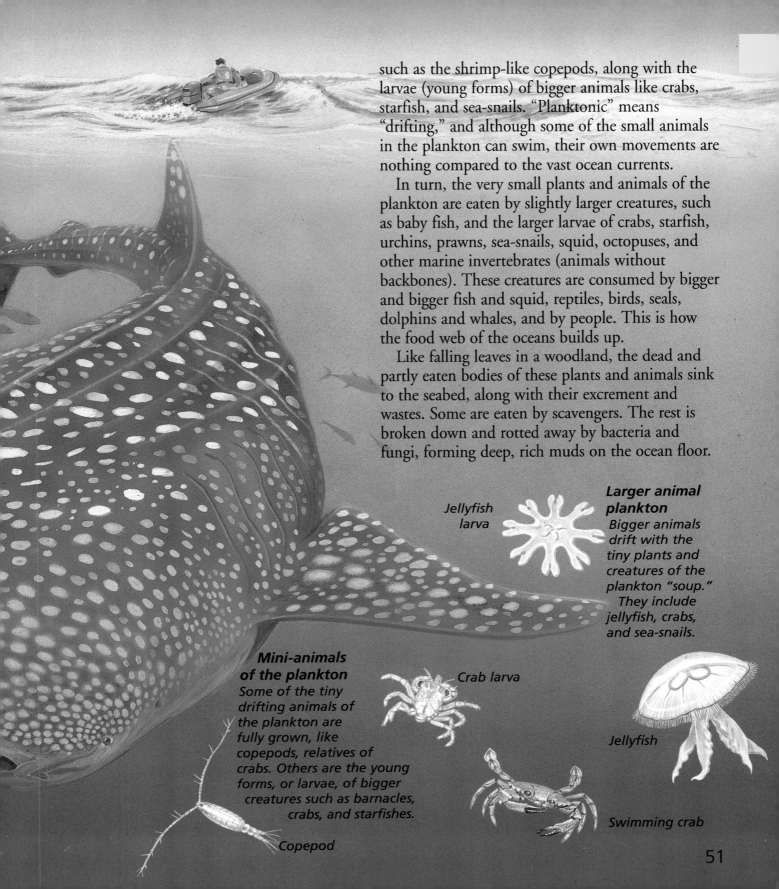

such as the shrimp-like copepods, along with the larvae (young forms) of bigger animals like crabs, starfish, and sea-snails. "Planktonic" means "drifting," and although some of the small animals in the plankton can swim, their own movements are nothing compared to the vast ocean currents.

In turn, the very small plants and animals of the plankton are eaten by slightly larger creatures, such as baby fish, and the larger larvae of crabs, starfish, urchins, prawns, sea-snails, squid, octopuses, and other marine invertebrates (animals without backbones). These creatures are consumed by bigger and bigger fish and squid, reptiles, birds, seals, dolphins and whales, and by people. This is how the food web of the oceans builds up.

Like falling leaves in a woodland, the dead and partly eaten bodies of these plants and animals sink to the seabed, along with their excrement and wastes. Some are eaten by scavengers. The rest is broken down and rotted away by bacteria and fungi, forming deep, rich muds on the ocean floor.

Jellyfish larva

Larger animal plankton
Bigger animals drift with the tiny plants and creatures of the plankton "soup." They include jellyfish, crabs, and sea-snails.

Mini-animals of the plankton
Some of the tiny drifting animals of the plankton are fully grown, like copepods, relatives of crabs. Others are the young forms, or larvae, of bigger creatures such as barnacles, crabs, and starfishes.

Crab larva

Jellyfish

Swimming crab

Copepod

51

Whales of the World

The wide-open ocean is home to the largest animal on Earth, the blue whale. Adults can grow to 100 feet, as long as a good-sized swimming pool! These huge animals used to be found worldwide, but because of human hunting, they are now rare. The best chance of seeing a blue whale is in the southern oceans around Antarctica, in summer—between December and February. Blues and many other whales gather here to feed on the immense swarms of krill, squid and other small creatures.

There are two main kinds of whale, the baleen (whalebone) and toothed whales. Baleen whales like the blue, fin, humpback, and minke whale sieve their food through a row of fringed, horny plates called "baleen." These hang like combs from the roof of the mouth. The whale takes in a giant mouthful of water, squeezes it out through the baleen so the small creatures are trapped inside the sieve, then licks them off and swallows them. A blue whale can eat four million krill each day, weighing about four tons!

Humpback
Whales and dolphins call in the water to mates, rivals, and neighbors. Humpback whales can hear each other's songs from hundreds of miles away.

Killer whale
Killer whales are not true whales, but the largest members of the dolphin group. They cooperate to hunt whales, seals, squid, fish, and sea birds.

Narwhal
This toothed whale has a unicorn-like tusk, which is one of its teeth that grows very long. Rival males fence with their tusks at mating time.

Beluga
A smallish, toothed whale 16.5 feet long, the beluga lives around the coasts of the North Atlantic and among Arctic icebergs.

Fin whale
The second-largest whale, 82 feet long and 77 tons in weight, a fin can swim faster, and for longer, than any of its cousins.

Bryde's whale
The most tropical of the big whales, Bryde's prefers the warm waters near the Equator. It was not really numerous or big enough to be worth hunting.

Right whale
This North Atlantic whale got its name from being the "right" whale to hunt in the days of whaling. It swam slowly, was big, with plenty of meat and oil, and it floated when harpooned and killed.

The toothed group of whales includes the sperm whale, narwhal, beluga, pilot whales, and the very deep-diving beaked whales. They have pointed teeth to grasp slippery prey like squid and fish.

Commercial hunting brought the great whales to the edge of extinction in less than 200 years. They were killed for oil, meat, and baleen. By the 1960s, some species were reduced to only a few hundred individuals. In 1986, nearly all the world's nations agreed to stop mass whaling. The numbers of some whales may be increasing. But these vast mammals grow and breed so slowly, it will probably take another century to make sure they are safe from extinction. The Southern Ocean around Antarctica has been declared one huge whale sanctuary.

Blue whale
The blue holds the record as the largest animal alive on Earth. As with most whales, females are slightly larger than males.

Sperm whale
The biggest of the toothed whales, the sperm is the world's largest carnivore. Big males reach 65 feet long.

The Dolphin's Day

Like their bigger relations the whales, and their tubbier relatives the porpoises, dolphins are mammals. They have warm blood and breathe air, but they have no fur. This has been lost over millions of years of evolution, although a few whales do have small whiskers around the snout. Whales, dolphins and porpoises all belong to the mammal group called cetaceans.

Dolphins are mainly hunters of the open ocean. They chase after fish, squid and other creatures, which they catch with their sharp, cone-shaped teeth. Cetaceans come to the surface regularly to breathe through their blowholes. These are really their nostrils, which have moved during evolution, from the tip of the snout to the top of the forehead. Dolphins and some whales find their way around using a type of sound-radar called "sonar" or "echolocation." (Bats do the same in the air.) They send out squeaks, clicks, and pulses of sound. These bounce off objects such as rocks and shoals of fish. The dolphin listens to the pattern of returning echoes, and works

Leaping about
Most dolphins are intelligent and playful. They swim and splash in the waves from boats, and they have never been known to harm people swimming with them. The bottlenose dolphin is sometimes seen performing in aquariums and sea-world centers.

54

out what is around it—even in dark, muddy water or at night. Unfortunately, we have made the sea a very noisy place. People use blasts of sound in their search for oil. Rare river dolphins suffer from loud boat traffic and so they get lost in the murky water. Some scientists want to experiment with very loud sounds that would travel right across an ocean. Others say this would disrupt and damage the lives of dolphins and whales.

Another danger is fishing. Vast, curtain-shaped nets are hung in the water to catch tuna and similar fish. But dolphins sometimes get trapped in them.

Smile of death
Dolphins look happy and playful to us, because of the natural "smiley" shape of their mouth. In reality they are voracious hunters, tearing up large prey and swallowing small victims whole— and alive.

Striped dolphin
This sleek sea mammal lives worldwide in warmer oceans, and grows about 8 feet long.

Common dolphin
Less common today, this is the dolphin pictured in murals and mosaics in Ancient Greece and Rome.

Bottlenose dolphin
One of the largest of the dolphin group, it grows to 13 feet long and lives in all warmer seas.

Dall's porpoise
Most porpoises live near the coast but Dall's porpoise, which is 6.5 feet long, dwells in the open ocean.

They cannot surface for air, so they suffocate and drown. These nets also kill turtles and seals in a similar way. Since the mass killing of large whales stopped, some dolphin species are now hunted commercially for meat and oil. Many are not protected by wildlife laws—as yet.

Sharks and Turtles

Only a few animals attack and eat people. Sharks are probably the most feared of all. However, we are much more dangerous to sharks than they are to us. About 30 people a year are killed by sharks. Yet people kill up to 100 million sharks every year. Sharks have the longest history of almost any group of fish. They have been around for over 400 million years, 200 million years before the dinosaurs.

Sharks are top predators and scavengers. They feed on sick and weak animals. Yet sharks are themselves in danger from over-fishing. They are killed for food and caught in fishing competitions. Most sharks do not lay lots of eggs, like other fish. Instead, the mother gives birth to a few young, called pups. If too many sharks are killed, the numbers take a long time to build up again. Scientists in Europe and America have recently formed a group to help "save the sharks."

Like sharks, turtles have been around since before the dinosaurs. All eight species of sea turtles are harmless and threatened with extinction. The biggest, the leatherback, wanders the world's warmer oceans, eating mainly jellyfish.

Mako shark

Sharks large and small
Sharks range in size from small, harmless dogfish to the dangerous great white sharks and hamerheads. Most hunt by smell, and can detect one drop of blood in a body of water the size of a swimming pool. Turtles are reptiles and so they must come to the surface to breathe air.

Loggerhead turtle

Thresher shark

Hammerhead
This extremely dangerous shark has eyes and nostrils on the ends of its wedge-like head.

Sandy dogfish
Dogfish are small members of the shark group. They eat shellfish, fish, worms, crabs, shrimps, and other types of prey.

Manta ray

This largest ray, one of the biggest fish, is nearly 23 feet wide. It "flies" through the water by flapping its wings, and filters plankton through its wide mouth.

Leatherback turtle

This sea reptile grows to 6 feet long and weighs 1,430 lbs. Its outer shell is not hard and rigid, but tough and leathery. It swims by rowing with its front legs.

THREATS TO SEA TURTLES

Many of the sandy beaches where sea turtles lay their eggs have now been changed into holiday resorts. Their eggs are taken by people and by animals such as lizards and gulls. Turtles are also killed for food and for their beautiful shells. They drown in nets and die from eating plastic bags that they mistake for jellyfish. Many countries have now banned the import of anything made from turtles. You can help by never buying turtle shell souvenirs.

Breeding on beaches

Sea turtles must return to land to breed. A green turtle lays her eggs in a hole on a sandy beach, then leaves them to develop and hatch by themselves.

Stingray

Named for the venomous spine on the underside of its tail, the stingray hides part-buried on the sea bed. It feeds mainly on shellfish, worms, and other bottom-dwelling creatures.

Great white

Also called the man-eater, this is the largest hunting shark, at 23 feet long. But it is becoming rare due to fishing and hunting, and is now a protected species in many areas.

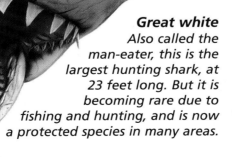

57

Seas of Seaweed

Large tree trunks, roots and branches can float down rivers and drift for thousands of miles across the sea. Animals and plants have adapted to these floating mini-habitats. Goose barnacles, seaweeds and sea firs settle and grow on them, and small fish, crabs, and shrimps find a home in this undergrowth. Shipworms, which are really a type of shellfish, were burrowing into driftwood long before they started attacking wooden ships. Wreckfish and even turtles follow the floating "raft," gaining shelter and food from this drifting mini-community of plants and animals. The world's biggest floating habitat is in the western North Atlantic Ocean. It is an area called the Sargasso Sea, near Bermuda. The water there is still and warm. Floating mats of seaweed grow thickly, undisturbed by any currents, and provide a vast, tangled raft for

A world of weed
The Sargasso Sea's floating rafts of seaweeds are home to many unique forms of life. Slow-moving animals protect themselves with hard shells, spines, and stings.

Eel nursery
Eels from European and North American rivers migrate to the Sargasso area, to spawn (lay eggs). It is thought that they do so at great depth, since they are found only very rarely in the floating weeds.

58

many fish, crabs, lobsters, shrimps, and sea snakes. Prickly sea urchins, limpets, and many kinds of sea-snails graze on the seaweeds.

Some of the Sargasso Sea's strangest fishes are frogfishes. Their fins look like legs, and they can waddle and hop among the fronds. Sea slugs are brightly colored relatives of garden slugs. But instead of munching lettuces, they graze the plant-like animals fixed to the seaweeds. Starfish may look slow and stupid, but they are ferocious predators. Even hard-shelled snails and bivalves such as mussels and clams are not safe. The starfish clamps the tiny, sucker-like tubes on its arms onto the two parts of the shell, and slowly pulls the shell halves apart to expose the animal inside. It then pushes its own stomach out through its mouth, and into the shell, and digests the flesh of the unfortunate victim.

Camouflage
Many Sargasso animals, like the frogfishes and seahorses, are decorated with flaps and tassels, for camouflage among the weed. They merge into the frilly background.

A MYSTERY SOLVED

For hundreds of years, no one in Europe or North America knew where freshwater eels came from. Then, in about 1910, it was discovered that mature eels swim out across the Atlantic, to the Sargasso Sea. They lay eggs deep in the water, which develop into flattened, leaf-like larvae. After drifting in currents for thousands of miles, over two or three years, the larvae reach America or Europe and change into adults.

Adult eel

Larval eel

How Plants Live

Plants get the energy to live and grow by trapping the light energy from the Sun. This process is called photosynthesis. During it, the plant takes in the gas carbon dioxide (CO_2) and gives off oxygen (O_2). For plants in air, we cannot see this happening. For water plants, we can sometimes see the oxygen given off, as small bubbles. This happens especially from the plants in a still pond, or rock pool on warm, sunny days. You can see it too.

You need some pondweed, a large bowl, some coins, a funnel, and a test-tube or a similar long, thin, open-ended tube. The funnel and tube must be transparent and colorless, so that light can reach the plant.

1 Fill the bowl about two-thirds full with clean water. Dip the funnel and tube under the surface so all the air bubbles out of them.

2 Carefully put the tube over the narrow end of the funnel. Tip both upside down. The funnel's wide end rests on the bowl and the tube's base sticks above the surface.

3 The tube should stay full of water. Tilt the funnel slightly and put some fresh, green, leafy pondweed underneath it. Sit the funnel on coins so water can circulate under it.

4 Put the bowl and all its contents in a bright, sunny, warm place. After a short time, bubbles should start forming on the weed's leaves.

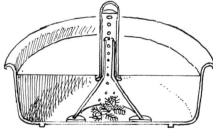

5 The bubbles float upwards. They are collected by the funnel and trapped in the tube. They are made of pure oxygen, from photosynthesis!

Some of the oxygen made by water plants becomes dissolved in the water. This dissolved oxygen is taken in or "breathed" by water animals, through their body surfaces or gills. So water plants are important for animal life in water—whether it is a home aquarium, a pond, a wide river, or the vast ocean.

Signs in Mud and Sand

The soft mud of a pondside, riverbank, or estuary, and the wet sand of a seashore, make excellent records of the animals who pass over them. There are footprints, tail drags, peck marks, and many other mysterious signs.

You can become a nature detective by studying the signs, sketching their shape, and measuring their size. See how many prints and other signs you can recognize, from those shown below and from the pictures in animal-tracking books. The sequence and the distance between footprints can show if the animal was walking, running, or leaping.

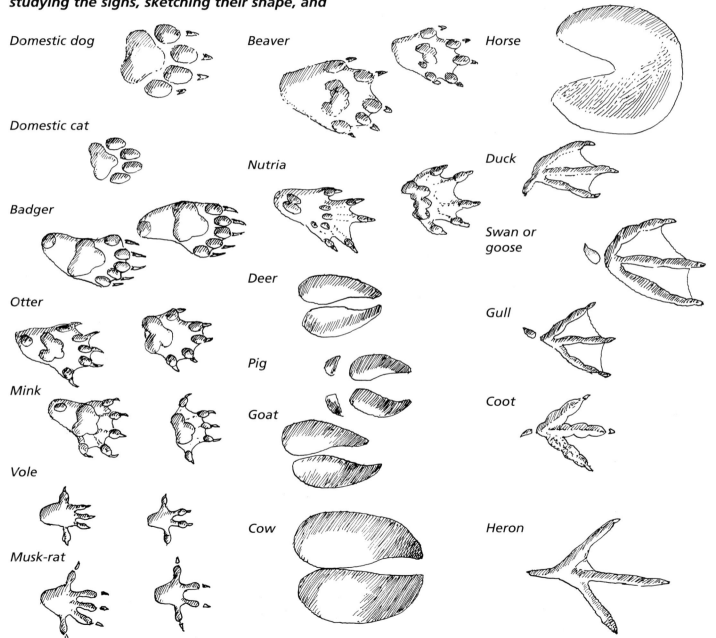

Domestic dog

Domestic cat

Badger

Otter

Mink

Vole

Musk-rat

Beaver

Nutria

Deer

Pig

Goat

Cow

Horse

Duck

Swan or goose

Gull

Coot

Heron

Oceans in Danger

The oceans are so vast, it may seem impossible that we can alter them. Yet even in the past thirty years, our use of the oceans has increased dramatically. We take more and more from the sea, and put back only our wastes and rubbish.

Fish, like herring and anchovies, live in big shoals, swimming in the open sea. By day they spread out and feed on plankton. At night the shoals pack tightly together, as their natural predators, such as tuna, sharks and sailfish, come up from the depths to feed on them. But their worst enemy is people. Giant trawlers find them by using sonar, and catch them in vast nets. So many were caught that hardly any remained. The numbers of herring fell so low that, in 1976, herring fishing was banned. Herring numbers are slowly increasing again.

The same is happening all over the world with dozens of fish species. Governments try to control

Anchovies and mackerel
These shoaling fish feed on plankton, and in turn become food for larger creatures. Mackerel swim inshore in summer, and to deeper waters in winter.

Tuna
A major food fish in warmer countries, tuna (below) have long, pointed fins and are speedy swimmers.

Atlantic cod
A large fish, 4 feet long, the cod is a predator of other fish and shellfish. These powerful swimmers move in large shoals near the surface.

Flatfish
Many other kinds of bottom-dwelling flatfish are caught for food.

Anchovy

Mackerel

over-fishing by allowing each country to catch only a certain amount and size of fish. This is called a quota. There are also rules about the sizes and types of nets. Modern monofilament drift nets are almost invisible in the water. In the eastern Pacific Ocean, yellow-fin tuna are caught by these nets. But the tuna fish live alongside dolphins. Fishermen use small aircraft to spot the dolphins and then set their nets in this area. The dolphins are caught with the tuna and many die by drowning. Whales, seals, and turtles are killed in the same way.

Some fishermen now use special nets with escape panels for the dolphins. Food containers labelled "dolphin-friendly" mean that the tuna or other fish have been caught in ways that do not harm dolphins. But on the remote high seas, it is very difficult to check every boat, or to catch illegal fishing fleets and prove their crimes. Also, the international laws about who can fish in which

Blue marlin
These huge, powerful fish are caught on rod and line for sport.

Fishing in past times
Up to about 1900, most fish was caught from small smacks like these (right) or from small trawlers. They only caught the large fish and so stocks were maintained.

Most of the seas that are rich in fish are fairly shallow, with ocean currents that bring plenty of nutrients. However, many of the traditional sites have now been "fished out." International laws do protect some of these areas, so the fish can breed and may be able to recover their numbers.

Factory ships
These modern trawlers catch every fish in the area in their huge nets. Only the smallest escape.

waters, and what they can catch there, are very complicated. Nations sometimes argue about fishing rights in the waters near their coasts. They may even send navy boats to protect their fleets and crews, and to stop rival boats ramming each other or cutting the lines of the other boats' nets.

Saving the Seas

Rivers and oceans are being harmed in many ways, besides over-fishing. Cutting down tropical rainforests can kill coral reefs! With the trees gone, the soil is washed by rain into the rivers. They carry the sediment to the sea, where it smothers the reefs. The corals and other fixed animals cannot run away or move out of the cloudy, polluted water.

With more people in the world, we are taking more and more food, minerals and other materials from the sea. Oil and gas are sucked from the seabed, but leaks and spills—some not so accidental—pollute huge areas and kill millions of sea creatures. Recently, some corals have been badly affected by disease, especially in the Caribbean Sea. This may be due to pollution. We are causing massive amounts of damage to our rivers, lakes, seas, and oceans—and it cannot continue.

PROTECTING OUR OCEANS

Marine nature reserves and parks are being set up around the world. Many were started by ordinary people who persuaded their governments that reserves are important. In some reserves, different activities are allowed in different areas. So fishermen, tourists, divers and scientists can all use the reserve without causing damage. This idea is called "zoning" and was first used in the Barrier Reef Marine Park in Australia.

Explosives
In parts of South-East Asia, fishermen illegally use dynamite to catch enough fish for their families. The explosions shatter coral, too.

Oil and gas
Oil and gas under the seabed are obtained by giant drilling platforms. These can work in water more than 350 feet deep and withstand hurricane-force winds.

Trawls
Fishing trawls plow up the seabed and smash many buried animals. In rich fishing grounds like the Irish Sea, it is now difficult to find any unplowed seabed.

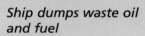
Ship dumps waste oil and fuel

Gill net

Fishing nets
Animals such as seals, whales, dolphins, manatees, and dugongs are mammals. They breathe air, like us. If they become tangled in the giant underwater nets meant for fish, they will drown.

Mass death
Trawls catch all kinds of sea animals, even very rare ones.

Trawl net

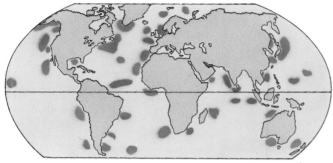

FLOATING GARBAGE

Even in the remotest parts of the ocean, garbage made of plastic, metal and glass bobs about on the waves or lies on the seabed. Most has been thrown overboard by passing ships. It is thought that the world's ships dump over six million tons of garbage into the sea every year.

How long will it last?
Cigarette end • 1–5 years
Orange peel • 2 years
Plastic bag • 10–20 years
Tin can • 50 years
Aluminium can • 80–100 years
Plastic bottle • 500 years
Glass bottle • 1 million years

Ecotourism

In Australia and other places, coral reefs are damaged by the many tourists who come to see them. In the growing business of ecotourism, swimming and scuba-diving must be carefully controlled. Tourist activity may also disturb rare creatures like the fur seals, which use the beaches for breeding. Some species of seals and sea lions are now very rare, and protected by law.

Industrial wastes

Containers of wastes are dumped on the seabed. They hold industrial chemicals, radioactive wastes, and even nerve gases and chemical weapons. Eventually the containers will rot and break. And then?

Purse-seine net

Underwater waste dump

Beachcomber's Collection

Beachcombing is great fun, and you'll find an endless variety of objects. Remember the sun can be very hot, so use a sun-screen cream, and take a T-shirt and hat. Read the Code of Safety on page 2 also!

1 Check tide times and visit the beach about two hours after high tide. A medium-sloping sandy beach is best. Walk slowly along the strand line where the high tide has left things stranded and drying. Never touch drums of chemicals, sewage or dead animals.

2 Gather any interesting items you find in a bucket, especially bones, feathers, shells, seaweeds, and pieces of wood. There are usually more things after stormy weather.

3 Back indoors, soak and clean the items thoroughly with fresh water and an old toothbrush. Identify them using seashore wildlife books and field guides. Group them into plants, molluscs, crabs, crustaceans, and so on.

4 Arrange the items on a piece of card or cotton wool for the box or tray. Painting shells with clear polyurethane varnish improves their colors and makes them look as though they have just come out of the water.

5 Label your finds with the place and time you found them, and their identity. If you can, visit the same beach in a different season, or again next year. Make another collection to compare the changes.

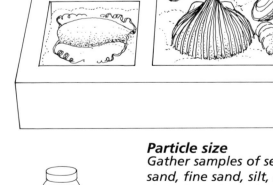

Particle size

Gather samples of seashore small pebbles, coarse sand, fine sand, silt, and mud. Put equal weights of these into clear plastic jars with equal volumes of water. Shake each jar well, and watch and time the speed of settling. Which one clears first? If you leave them, which dries out first? If you were a sea animal, which particles would you like to live among?

Survival in Rivers and Oceans

The best idea is: Do not get into trouble in the water in the first place. This means you should be properly dressed and prepared, with a life-jacket and other safety equipment.

Remember, in most parts of the world that the water in rivers, lakes, and seas is cold. It soon saps your body warmth and strength, making you tired and confused. Take care at all times, and think "Safety first" (see opposite contents page).

Banks and shores

Take care on riverbanks, near cliffs, and on rocky shores. They may be slippery or crumbly. Beware wet sand and mud: you could get stuck or sink in deep. On any sea coast, make sure the incoming tide will not cut you off.

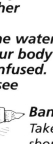

Waves and currents

Obey warning flags telling you not to swim. Avoid waves that could knock you over and make you very tired. Also avoid strong currents that might sweep you away. You can feel the undertow or see water swirling around buoys or other fixed objects. Make sure currents do not sweep you along the beach as you play and swim.

Shark menace

Do not panic and thrash about, as this may attract the shark. Swim slowly and regularly, backwards if you can, to watch the animal at all times. Shout loudly or beat the water regularly. The shark may give a test-nudge before attacking; hit or kick its snout as hard as possible.

In the water

Grab anything that helps you stay afloat, such as a paddle, float, piece of wreckage or even driftwood. Float on your back with legs apart, sculling with your hands, or tread water as if cycling slowly.

Move and breathe slowly to conserve energy. Remove heavy items like boots, but retain clothing for warmth. Signal for help by waving one arm straight, from side to side.

Rescue

If you see someone in trouble in the water, do not be tempted to leap in. It may be cold, with strong currents, and you'd also be in trouble. Look for a life-jacket, ring or rope, and get help by the fastest way possible (lifesavers, look-outs, phone, coastguard.)

Amazing Facts

OCEANS, SEAS AND LAKES

- **The area covered by all the seas and oceans of the world (called the hydrosphere) is about 139,782,000 square miles, which is almost exactly 71 per cent of the planet's total surface.**

- **All the world's oceans and seas contain 330 million cubic miles of salt water, most of it is in the southern hemisphere.**

- **The average depth of all the seas and oceans is 12,235 feet.**

The smallest sea is the St. Lawrence Gulf at 92,000 square miles. The Aral Sea in Uzbekistan is only 24,900 sq. miles, but since it is entirely surrounded by land, it is considered to be a lake rather than a sea.

The smallest and shallowest ocean is the Arctic. It covers 5.5 million sq. miles, and its average depth is 4,750 feet.

Lake Baikal in Russia is the deepest lake in the world at 5,7080 feet. It holds 20 per cent of the world's fresh, liquid (not frozen) water.

Lake Superior in North America has the largest surface area, 32,000 sq. miles, of any lake in the world.

The largest and deepest ocean is the Pacific. It covers 64 million sq. miles, 46 per cent of the world's total ocean surface, and its average depth is 14,100 feet.

The deepest part of any ocean is the Mariana Trench in the north-west, Pacific. The part called the Challenger Deep plunges to 36,160 feet below sea level. The summit of Mount Everest is 29,029 feet above sea level.

The largest sea is the Coral Sea at 1,850,000 sq. miles. Next is the South China Sea at 1,148,500 sq. miles.

RIVERS AND WAVES

Water flows over the Nakwakto rapids in Canada at 19 miles per hour, the strongest current in the world.

The greatest tidal range is in the Bay of Fundy, north-east America. The difference between high and low tides is 47.5 feet.

The world's third longest river is the Mississippi, at 3,740 miles.

The highest waterfall in the world is the Angel Falls in Venezuela, where the water of the River Carrao falls 2,650 feet in one leap, and 3,200 feet in total.

The Amazon River of South America, is the second longest river in the world, at 4,080 miles. But it contains more water than the other six biggest rivers in the world added together. It empties 4,240,000 cubic feet of water every second into the Atlantic Ocean, a flow 60 times that of the Nile. This huge amount of water is drained from the largest river basin in the world, 2,720,000 square miles.

A 50-foot tsunami that began in Portugal in 1755 killed 60,000 people in Western Europe, Morocco, and the West Indies.

There are bore waves—mini tidal waves flowing upstream—on about 60 rivers in the world. At spring tides on the Qiantong Jiang river in China, a wave 25 feet high travels along the river at about 15 miles per hour.

The highest tsunami (wave caused by seismic events) ever reported was in 1771, in the Ryukyu Islands. It was possibly 280 feet high.

The highest wave caused by weather conditions was in 1933, when a hurricane near the Philippines produced waves 112 feet high.

In 1883, a tsunami started in the Sunda Strait of South-East Asia. It reached 115 feet high and killed 36,000 people in Java and Sumatra.

A "river" flows hundreds of feet under the Pacific Ocean, eastward along the Equator. Called the Cromwell Current, it is 185 miles wide and 4,050 miles long.

The Boyoma Falls in Zaïre carry the greatest regular amount of water of any waterfall, at a rate of 600,400 cubic feet per second. The flow rate of the widest falls in the world, the Khône Falls in Laos (6.7 miles wide) rises temporarily to 1,500,000 cubic feet per second during floods.

The longest river in the world is the Nile of north-eastern Africa, at 4,157 miles.

A hidden river flows through the ground beneath the River Nile. It is thought to carry six times as much water as the river that flows above it.

The greatest current in the world flows around Antarctica at a rate of 4,600 million cubic feet of water per second.

Find Out More

The best place to begin your search for more information is your school library. Another excellent source of information is your public library. Most newspapers carry regular reports of new advances in science each week. For more information about plants and animals in this book, check with your nearest natural history museum. We have listed below a selection of books, organizations, videos, and multimedia programs that will help you learn more about OCEANS AND RIVERS.

GENERAL INFORMATION

Acid Rain Foundation
 1410 Varsity Drive,
 Raleigh, NC 27606
 919-828-9443
Adopt-a-Stream Foundation
 P.O. Box 5558 , Everett,
 WA 98206
 206-388-3313
American Cetacean Society
 P.O. Box 2639,
 San Pedro, CA 90731
 310-548-6279
American Rivers, Inc.
 801 Pennsylvania Avenue SE,
 Suite 303
 Washington, DC 20003-2167
 202-547-6900
American Shore & Beach Preservation
 c/o Gary Woodell
 13837 Fiji Way
 Marina Del Ray
 CA 90292
Atlantic Center for the Environment
 55 South Main

Ipswich, MA 01938
 508-356-0038
Center for Marine Conservation
 1725 DeSales Street NW,
 Suite 500
 Washington, DC 20036
 202-429-5609
Clean Water Action
 1320 18th Street, NW
 Washington DC 20036
 202-457-1286
Cousteau Society
 930 W. 21st Street, Norfolk, VA 23517
 804-627-1144
Ducks Unlimited
 1 Waterfowl Way,
 Long Grove, IL 60047
 312-438-4300
Freshwater Foundation
 2500 Shadywood Road, Box 90
 Navarre, MN 55392
 612-471-8407
Friends of the Sea Otter
 Box 221220, Carmel, CA 93922
 408-625-3290
Marine Mammal Stranding Center
 P.O. Box 733
 Brigantine, NJ 08203
 609-266-0538
National Audubon Society
 950 Third Avenue
 New York, NY 10022
 212-832-3200
National Geographic Society
 17th and M Streets, NW
 Washington, DC 20036
 202-857-7000
National Wildlife Federation
 1400 16th Street NW
 Washington, DC 20036
 202-797-6800
The Nature Conservancy
 1815 N. Lynn Street
 Arlington, VA 22209
 703-841-5300
North American Lake Management
 Society, P.O. Box 217
 Merrifield, VA 22116
 202-466-8550

Sierra Club
 100 Bush Street
 San Francisco, CA 94104
 415-291-1600
World Wildlife Fund
 1250 24th Street NW
 Washington, DC 20037
 202-293-4800

BOOKS

The Audubon Society Field Guide to North American Fishes, Whales and Dolphins
 Audubon Society Staff, et. al.
 Knopf/Random House
 ISBN 0-394-53405-0
Coral Reefs Sylvia Johnson
 Lerner Associates
 ISBN 0-8225-9545-1
The Dying Sea Michael Bright
 Franklin Watts
 ISBN 0-531-17126-4
Ecology Projects for Young Scientists
 Martin J. Gutnik
 Franklin Watts ISBN 0-531-04765-2
The Mysterious Undersea World.
 [Books *for World Explorers Series*]
 Jan Leslie Cook, National Geographic
 ISBN 0-97044-317-8

VIDEOS

National Geographic Society
 produces a wide range of wildlife and geographical videos
Time-Life Video
 produces a wide range of wildlife and geographical videos

MULTIMEDIA

3D Atlas Electronic Arts
The Big Green Disc Gale Research
Eyewitness Encyclopedia of Nature
 Dorling Kindersley
Global Learning Mindscape
Multimedia Animals Encyclopedia
 Applied Optical Media
Picture Atlas of the World
 National Geographic Society
Survey of the Animal Kingdom
 Zane Publishing
A World Alive Softline

Glossary

abyssal zone The deepest parts of the ocean, below about 6,500 feet, which are usually completely dark.

bathyal zone The parts of lakes and oceans between about 670 and 6,500 feet, the 'twilight zone' where some sunlight penetrates.

breaker A wave that builds up and topples over or "breaks" as a foaming mass, as it approaches shallower water.

continental drift The movement of the main continents or landmasses around the surface of the Earth, carried on TECTONIC PLATES.

current A body or volume of water that moves in relation to the water around it.

delta Found at the ESTUARY or mouth of a river where it flows into the sea, and where the river usually divides and splits into many smaller waterways that flow through a large triangle-shaped area of mud, sand or similar land.

estuary The mouth of a river, where it usually becomes wider as it flows into the sea.

evaporation When a liquid turns into a vapor or gas. Liquid water evaporates or "dries" into invisible water vapor.

food chain A list or sequence of who eats what, beginning with plants and ending with the top carnivore. In nature, many food chains usually link to form food webs.

habitat A type of place or surroundings in the natural world, often named after the main plants that grow there. Examples are a conifer forest, a grassland such as a meadow, a desert, a pond or a sandy seashore. Some animals are adapted to only one habitat, like limpets on rocky seashores. Other animals, like foxes, can survive in many habitats.

hydrothermal vent A crack or hole, usually on the seabed, through which very hot water gushes from deep below the surface.

lithospheric plate See TECTONIC PLATE.

neap tide The smallest tidal range, where the high tide is quite low and the low tide is relatively high. Compare SPRING TIDE.

mid-oceanic ridge A strip of raised sea bed, like a line of underwater hills or mountains, usually between two TECTONIC PLATES. New seabed is formed here as rocks well up from deep in the Earth and the plates slide away from each other.

plankton Mass of small plants (phytoplankton) and animals (zooplankton) drifting near the surface of seas or lakes.

precipitation The overall name for water reaching the surface of the Earth, which includes rain, sleet, snow, frost and dew.

salinity The measure of saltiness or salt content (in sea water, this is mainly common or sea or table salt, sodium chloride).

spring tide The biggest tidal range, where the high tide is very high and the low tide is very low. Compare NEAP TIDE.

surface zone The parts of lakes and oceans down to about 670 feet, where plenty of sunlight penetrates.

tectonic plate One of the giant curved plates that makes up the outer surface of the Earth, and which moves or drifts in relation to the other plates. (Also called lithospheric plate.)

tsunami Large wave and water currents produced by earthquake activity. Although it is sometimes called a "tidal wave," it has nothing to do with tides.

Index